Injustice for All

Injustice for All

The (Familiar) Fallacies of Criminal Justice Reform

Brian Surber

TRUEBLUE
publishing
Broken Arrow, Oklahoma

Published by True Blue Publishing LLC
2320 W Waco Street
Broken Arrow, Oklahoma 74011, USA

Copyright 2021 by Brian Surber

Printed in the United States of America on acid-free paper

ISBN-13: 978-1-7367421-1-2 (hbk)
ISBN-13: 978-1-7367421-0-5 (pbk)
ISBN-13: 978-1-7367421-2-9 (ebk)

Library of Congress Control Number: 2021904655

Cover design by Lydia Surber

To Lynel, Jacob, Lydia and Jonah . . . my World,
To my parents . . . for EVERYTHING,
To every other Surber, Cuttler, Novak, Beck,
and Widowski . . . I love you all,
To every victim . . . you will never be a number to Us.

Contents

Preface

The Case for Enforcement

Criminal justice reform—this innocuous-sounding phrase is, in reality, a cloak for one of the greatest threats to the internal safety of the United States. I have been in law enforcement for nearly a quarter century as a prosecutor, general counsel for a police agency, and narcotics agent. Throughout that time, I have noticed that many people from many disciplines have a great deal of input on just how to deal with criminals. Whether social scientists, academics, think tanks, committees, legislators, or media pundits, those entities seeking changes to how police and prosecutors deal with criminals almost invariably comprise individuals who have virtually no experience in law enforcement. Police officers and prosecutors do not write letters telling treatment professionals how to conduct their work, but the criminal justice system repeatedly gets unsolicited input from a multitude of sources. To be sure, present-day America is experiencing a growing onslaught of initiatives aimed at drastically changing the enforcement of our criminal laws, all of which only serve to hobble law enforcement.

In a way, the last several years have been maddening. Only a few years ago, these theories would have been overwhelmingly viewed with disdain—considered the dogma of left-wing groups like the American Civil Liberties Union or the National Organization for the Reform of Marijuana Laws. For instance, one absurd but popular theory is that people would steal less if only the penalty were reduced to hardly any penalty at all. Amazingly, what drug and property crime America experienced was actually attributed to the penalties resulting from its commission. My boss, Matt Ballard, District Attorney for the Twelfth District of Oklahoma, keenly and succinctly summarized the theory as follows:

> It's as if there are a bunch of people speeding in my neighborhood, everyone complains about the speeders, and the police keep having to write tickets. Rather than targeting those that break the law, officials target the laws and those enforcing the law. To fix the problem, we just raise the speed limit—sure, less people will speed, but the streets are far from safer.

Having worked in government, it is hard to advocate for its efficiency. As such, I have always been a fan of economists who argue for the limited role of government, such as Frederick Hayek, Milton Friedman, and Thomas Sowell. Other contemporary figures influencing what could be called libertarian ideals are too numerous to mention. Traditionally, those on the so-called left and right view the world very differently—one placing faith in government and the other advocating for governmental restraint, and each having its vocational advocates. But rarely, if ever, have these polar opposite ideologies shared foundational beliefs—until now.

Having spent my entire career in law enforcement, predominantly drug enforcement, I have seen the devastation drugs cause. I have observed firsthand how the assumptions surrounding the narratives of criminal justice reform were far removed from reality. Consequently, I was dismayed at the traction these reform movements were getting due in large part to people who held basic beliefs very similar to my own. In fact, the overwhelming majority of law enforcement professionals believe in limited government, so the fallacies of criminal justice reform were a source of constant frustration—and bewilderment.

Then I was on vacation and bought a copy of Fredrick Hayek's *The Road to Serfdom*. I was familiar with Hayek, having viewed decades-old videos of his lectures on YouTube, and I had heard of *The Road to Serfdom*. Hayek was writing his book to document how much of mid-century Western society was endangering its prosperity by endorsing ideas from socialist ideologies, birthed from intellectuals, that also found favor in the media and entertainment industry. As I read Hayek's work and considered the political debate currently taking place in the United States, it was as if Hayek were writing his book in 2020—like all great philosophers, his writings appeared timeless. But, as I read *The Road to Serfdom,* the players, the settings, the methods, all sounded familiar. The debate over economic policy completely mirrored the debate over policing and drug enforcement.

Hayek never mentioned drug legalization, but the most influential libertarian of the twentieth century, Milton Friedman, did. In fact, Friedman advocated for the complete legalization of narcotics, and he was not alone among small-government economic theorists. I was now more perplexed than ever as to how such brilliant individuals could argue for the decriminalization of drugs or other aspects of criminal justice enforcement.

On that vacation, while enjoying a margarita with my wife, I told her of my thoughts regarding Hayek's work as it related to contemporary criminal justice reform efforts. She encouraged me to write a book, and we agreed I would start it immediately. I will forever be grateful for her constant support in this endeavor from that day forward. It was an anniversary trip—at a cabin in the woods. The surroundings of the forest in the fall provided the perfect setting for me to get up the next morning and begin to outline the contents of the book. And so it began. I began to focus my spare time on studying the evolution of small-government (perhaps libertarian) thought, and the more I read, the more apparent became the reasons small-government advocates should support the enforcement of drug laws and laws against so-called nonviolent crimes.

Ironically, I did not have to counter their positions but merely employ them. In fact, I have learned and continue to learn a great deal from the works of those economic philosophers who argue for a limited government in the interest of individual liberty. While at times I will address an unequivocal statement from one or more of these thinkers and make every effort to dismantle it at the core, I mean no disrespect. These giants of economic policy simply did not have real experience with the drug addict, criminal enterprises, or the habitual offender. To be sure, it is the influence and rationale of the small-government movement that has enabled me to outline just why a libertarian should be ardently in favor of prohibiting the use of narcotics and enforcement efforts aimed at halting the same.

I cite a number of references throughout the book. However, five works that I have read multiple times had a profound intellectual impact on me, and I must acknowledge them separately, while also ardently recommending these books for everyone to read. First, the aforementioned *The Road to Serfdom* by Frederick Hayek began a revolution in thought and is as brilliant today as it was in the 1940s. Second, *On Dope—Drug Enforcement and the First Policeman* by Jeffrey B. Stamm is a tremendous historical treatise on the importance of drug enforcement. Third, *Tell Your Children the Truth about Marijuana, Mental Illness, and Violence* by Alex Berenson brilliantly unpacks the fraud of the medical marijuana movement with the historical record, a slew of academic studies, and contemporary examples, all of which destroy the prevailing cultural narrative surrounding cannabis. Also, *The War on Cops* by Heather MacDonald is an absolute wrecking ball to the false narratives perpetuated about police. Finally, *Intellectuals and Society* by Thomas Sowell is a masterpiece that demonstrates the damage the intellectual class has done to Western society in economic policy, race relations, national defense, and the application of the law, and without question, this treatise provides incalculable insight into the negative influence of the "intelligentsia" on criminal justice reform.

Finally, I must acknowledge my brothers and sisters in law enforcement. It would be an impossible task to include all of those law enforcement professionals who have influenced me, but I am compelled to mention a few. District Attorney Robert Schulte, and his prosecutors, inspired me to become a prosecutor after working for him in law school; the late Lisa Goodspeed influenced me from my first day as a sworn assistant district attorney; Mark Gibson treated me like his younger brother and taught me how to prosecute DUIs and death penalty cases; OBN director Lonnie Wright's belief in me I will never forget; Scott Rowland is the most intelligent attorney I have ever encountered; OBN director Darrell Weaver allowed me to become a narcotics agent at the Bureau; Travis White's skill as a drug prosecutor, agency attorney, teacher, and leader cannot be articulated (and I am very lucky Travis is my best friend, as every time we talk, I get smarter); the entirety of the Association of Oklahoma Narcotic Enforcers and its executive board have supported me throughout my career; District Attorney Matt Ballard is a tremendous leader, prosecutor, and friend, as without him, I would not be where I am today; investigator Wayne Stinnett's counsel and excellence continually propel me forward; and I could not have become who I am today without all of the professional law enforcement associations (especially the leadership thereof) with which I have had the privilege to collaborate and all of the leaders who I can only attempt to emulate, especially Special Agent in Charge Richard Salter. Thanks also to the rest of those law enforcement professionals who have taught me so much—if we have talked, emailed, or texted, I mean you. In the fight to protect the public, I have been privileged to serve with you. The fight has never been more daunting, but I damn sure like my team.

Introduction

Recently, social justice intellectuals on the left and those with a libertarian perspective on the right have been pushing for an odd marriage of "criminal justice reform." The misunderstandings and misguided principles as well as the false narratives supporting this effort are the subject of this book. *Enforcement* as used in this book encompasses several activities—it includes the existence (or nonexistence) of particular laws, the actual enforcement of those laws, and the subsequent prosecution of those offenses.

There has been no greater target of criminal justice reform than the enforcement of narcotics laws. However, decades upon decades of historical evidence has related to the need for the Uniform Controlled Dangerous Substance Act (the basic structure of the federal and state drug laws in the United States) and the importance of enforcing what some describe as "low-level" offenses. But much more importantly, the disastrous track record of society's periodic initiatives aimed at restricting the enforcement of these laws is not only compelling but unassailable. The comparison of this history of enforcement to periodic efforts aimed at reducing enforcement, including very recent examples, is a major aim of this book.

Many of the most influential libertarians and conservatives started on the left, or perhaps even as socialists (Hayek, Friedman, and Sowell themselves, along with Ronald Reagan, Charles Krauthammer, Dave Rubin, and

Candace Owens, to name only a few). When these thinkers are asked what caused their evolution in belief, the response is almost always that they were persuaded by evidence. It is exactly this allegiance to evidence and reason that should convince any individual as to the need for enforcement of our criminal laws, especially those self-described libertarians and small-government conservatives. In fact, it is my absolute hope—actually, my expectation—that these libertarians and conservatives who arrived at their core beliefs through examining and evaluating facts and evidence will come not only to understand the need for dedicated enforcement of property and drug crimes but ardently to support the same.

Thomas Sowell masterfully differentiates between the practices of intellectuals and the realization of actual wisdom. He describes an intellectual as someone whose occupation deals with ideas, yet who does not have any past experience or current obligation to put the ideas into practice—a policy wonk. In contrast, Sowell says, "wisdom is the rarest quality of all—the ability to combine intellect, knowledge, experience, and judgment in a way to produce a coherent understanding."[1] While the ultimate objective of this book is to advocate for public policy, it does so from the perspective of wisdom. This book contains the intellect, knowledge, experience, and judgment required for Sowell's definition of wisdom.

It is quite understandable how many libertarians came not only to be suspect of enforcing narcotics laws but openly to advocate for the laws' decriminalization or outright repeal. As such, the following chapters not only examine how libertarians honestly came to question narcotics laws but also illustrate how enforcement of drug laws (and so-called nonviolent offenses) is actually essential to libertarian beliefs and objectives relating to the role of government. To do so, it will be important to discuss exactly why government exists at all—that is, what exactly is the State, what forms does the State take, and what are the possible roles of the State?

If anyone should be suspicious of arguments pushed by social justice advocates in support of criminal justice reform, it should be libertarians and conservatives. In fact, a closer examination of this movement demonstrates not just the well-merited skepticism of the criminal justice reform messengers but also that the messaging techniques those on the left use to promote decriminalizing narcotics laws and other criminal justice reform measures are nearly identical to the methods the intellectual left uses to argue for the expanded and exploded role of government—even socialism. Curiously enough, many of the same factors that continue to account for the growing popularity of socialism have likewise contributed to the growing popularity of criminal justice reform.

This book also summarizes the history and experience of both criminal justice enforcement and the lack thereof. The results are compelling—actually, alarming. Finally, this book examines the effectiveness of the proposed alternatives to enforcement and demonstrates that such efforts are no substitute for the effectiveness of enforcement.

It is this historical record, as well as the collective knowledge and experience of law enforcement, that demonstrates the importance of enforcement not only under libertarian principles but for anyone interested in the condition of society, regardless of his or her political ideology. This book is not simply for the ardent libertarian. American culture is fast approaching a precipice. In fact, it may be more accurate to say that our society has already begun the slide. So, who can gain insight from the book? Advocates against child abuse and neglect, individuals worried about the homelessness crisis, people concerned about domestic violence, educators who want our students to perform better, those who help persons afflicted with mental health problems, fiscal hawks who bemoan government expenditures, and parents who want the best America for their children and grandchildren all have a stake in the costs of failing to adequately enforce our drug and property crimes. In fact, if you live in America, this book is for you.

The Purpose of the State

Mankind has survived, even thrived, for tens of thousands of years because of cooperation between people in groups. The State has existed much longer than "civilization" itself. In fact, as long as humans have lived together, the State has existed. A tribe of cave dwellers working toward the tribe's survival is a form of the State. The State can serve a multitude of functions, and those functions can be illustrated by contemplating the most primitive of cavemen or even a modern industrialized nation.

First, the State must preserve itself from external threats. For the cavemen, that function would be some sort of coordinated effort aimed at protecting the band from predatory animals or perhaps a warring band. In a modern nation-state, the protection of external threats is accomplished by maintaining a military force.

Next, the State must maintain some internal order. For a primitive tribe, that order could be achieved by establishing a simple set of rules regarding prohibited conduct or assignment of duties. In a modern nation, that order is achieved by a drafted code of conduct, mechanisms for enforcing those rules, and consequences for violations of the rules (i.e., laws, policing, and criminal punishments, respectively).

After security from the outside is established and there is order among the group, the State next must concern itself with considerations of the public good. These concerns could be as simple as care for elder members of the tribe or as complicated as an entire health care system for a modern country. What qualifies as the public good and by what measures that public good is achieved have been contemplated, debated, and warred over for millennia.

The entire genre of movies and books describing a postapocalyptic world (whether a nuclear holocaust or zombie pandemic) demonstrates our human fascination with the creation of the State. Humans can contemplate the absence of order and immediately relate to the primal desire for protection from external threats, and such fiction also provides us with compelling thought regarding the challenges of creating and maintaining internal rules for the group—the first and second functions of the State.

As a modern-day, yet primitive, example, among large groups of incarcerated men, any observer can see the formation of a type of State. Associations in prison are typically made along racial lines—perhaps due to some primitive form of tribal instinct. Once these competing factions (i.e., prison gangs) are formed, their first objective is to protect their members from other prisoners. Also during formation, the gangs create a set of rules to maintain the cohesiveness of the group, and violations of these rules are met with brutal violence. In an effort to maintain order, agreements between gangs, which resemble treaties, are created to further protect the groups. Among the main provisions of the agreements is the prohibition of one gang's membership killing a member of another gang, unless permission is granted by the latter gang's leadership—obviously to avoid unnecessary conflict or warfare among the gangs. Once structured, the gangs then engage in commerce. In prison, food and shelter are provided, so the main commodities in prison are contraband, such as drugs, cigarettes, alcohol, and cellular telephones. The prison gangs therefore oversee smuggling of contraband within the prison and the placement of money on commissary accounts, oftentimes by family members placing money on these accounts as payment for the contraband, with the leadership receiving the bulk of the proceeds. In a way, these commissary accounts act as a banking system for prison commerce. A simple observation of our most deviant citizens provides much insight into the formation of the State.

Various models of government constituting the State have been tried for as long as the State has existed. Some represent a philosophy as to what constitutes the best civilization, and some are merely a method of maintaining order among the members to achieve the objectives of the State. These objectives and the methods of achieving them can be decided by the members themselves (as in some form of democracy), by a single individual (like a monarchy or dictatorship), or by a group of elites (an aristocracy, for instance). These variances in both the objectives and methods to achieve them have resulted in drastically different models of government. From collectivist to individualist, totalitarian to anarchy, libertarian to socialist, all forms of government represent some form of an idea regarding what is best for the particular society.

Even the aspects of external and internal security are the subject of contentious argument to this very day. For instance, although the need for American national security is not disputed, what constitutes a national security threat and how many national resources to expend toward maintaining a standing, war-ready military in the United States are subjects of constant debate. Likewise, what domestic laws are needed, how those laws are to be enforced, what policing practices are appropriate, and what to do with those who violate the law are even more debated in modern-day America, and with much more vitriol. But we must distinguish between the unassailable core functions of the State (external and internal security) and the goals of the State. Virtually every human will agree that his or her group cannot be overrun by a hostile competing group. While the methods to achieve this external security and the resources devoted to this security are the subject of much disagreement, external security itself is not. Likewise, virtually no one seriously argues that any collection of people, large or small, can function without a set of rules outlining acceptable conduct. Despite the constant vigorous debate regarding both what those rules should be and the consequences for violations thereof, the need for rules and enforcement is the foundation for each of the various beliefs.

However, the actual goals of the State, beyond these two core functions, have not been the concern merely of philosophers; virtually any governed person has a belief about that toward which his or her society should be working. More complicated still, those who agree on the goals of the State oftentimes have less agreement regarding what governmental model will best achieve those goals. Jean-Jacques Rousseau wrote an influential book titled *The Social Compact*. And while Rousseau's book examines the historical examples of nations and their governments, it is in the end a treatise on the best form of the State. The same could be said of Machiavelli's *The Prince*. It is no wonder that politics has no place at the family dinner table.

As I outline in the next chapter, libertarians believe in very little government intervention in economic and social affairs, while socialists believe in a centralized government directing the affairs of society. In fact, while a libertarian may support the function of a government, he or she may believe that the State need only protect personal liberty and that attempts at effecting social policy inevitably lead to infringements on liberty or even tyranny. But simply stating the basic tenets of a small-government libertarian does not elucidate the reasoning supporting such beliefs and has certainly contributed to a sect of conservatives supporting the legalization of drugs and the decriminalization of other offenses. It is now time to examine the reasoning supporting these core libertarian beliefs.

The Evolution of Small-Government and Libertarian Thought

Prelude to Libertarian Thought

To be sure, religion, agriculture, science, and a multitude of other factors have impacted the formation of all stages of society. Likewise, a mere summary of the history of thought among philosophers on the proper form of the State would fill up shelves at a library. But only a few such thinkers are mentioned here—those who have most influenced small-government beliefs in our nation today. These summaries of small-government philosophy, which are brief indeed, are included not to persuade the reader but rather to explain why a libertarian or small-government advocate may question narcotics laws and other criminal justice enforcement—and to form the foundation as to why those who subscribe to such beliefs should support vigorous enforcement of these laws.

Modern libertarian philosophy was certainly influenced by seventeenth-century thought. While Thomas Hobbes believed that man has the fundamental natural right to do anything he pleases, Hobbes recognized that man at his core is ferocious. As a result, Hobbes argued for an absolute ruler and provided a philosophical justification for a monarchy. Hobbes believed that even the injustices of the individual ruler are better than the original condition of man.[1]

In contrast to Hobbes, John Locke believed that the original state of man was peaceful and that man naturally moves toward society and mutual assistance. Locke opposed any monarchy and believed that the will of the majority (represented in law) should rule society. To that end, Locke argued that the purpose of the law is to preserve the social group and that the law must limit itself to the public good of society. Locke also believed that those who drafted the laws should not be the ones to enforce those laws, which had a strong influence on America's principle of the separation of powers.[2]

The next influence in the evolution of libertarian thought was the formation of the doctrine of laissez-faire. This economic term was coined by a group of French economic thinkers known as Physiocrats. Laissez-faire theory holds that an uncontrolled economy actually produces order, not chaos, and that the State should not interfere in the affairs of its members any more than is absolutely necessary. That is, the best form of government is one in which each individual has the natural right to exercise his or her affairs (i.e., labor) in the economic realm with the least possible interference from the State, and everything the individual obtains is his or hers alone.[3]

But perhaps no writing had more impact on the birth of economic libertarian ideals than Adam Smith's *Wealth of Nations,* which was written during this new era of economic thought, and writings of the laissez-faire Physiocrats. For thousands of years, philosophers had urged that the purpose of the State was to regulate most of the activities of man, yet Smith's written vision of the ideal government was premised on the State's restraint. In fact, Smith believed that the State should make efforts toward a hands-off approach and limit its existence to situations in which the safety of the society was threatened. To that end, *Wealth of Nations* also urged that the ideal State was one in which individuals engaged in free exchange and unrestricted competition. Thomas Sowell summarized Smith's argument for governmental restraint articulated in the *Wealth of Nations* as follows:

> To those with this vision [of a hands-off approach by government], for the authorities to impose economic policies would be to give "a most unnecessary attention," in Adam Smith's words, to a spontaneous system of interactions that would go better without government intervention—not perfectly, just better.[4]

However, not long after Smith's beliefs gained a following, a different and diametrically opposed belief system urging a much more central role of the State emerged. This opposing belief system was influenced by Georg Wilhelm Friedrich Hegel and ultimately the man so influential on collectivist thought that an entire philosophy became his namesake—Karl Marx.[5]

While Adam Smith's *Wealth of Nations* continues to be influential on issues of economic liberty, perhaps no writing has had a greater impact on the notion of personal liberty than John Stuart Mill's *On Liberty,* which was published in 1859. Mill's opening sentence outlines his purpose: "The subject of this Essay is . . . the nature and limits of the power which can be legitimately exercised by society over the individual."[6] With respect to a government's effort to enact laws to protect the individual, Mill stated, "All errors which he is likely to commit against advice and warning, are far outweighed by the evil of allowing others to constrain him to what they deem his good."[7] Without question, Mill is an ardent advocate of personal liberty, and he argues for the same not simply for the individual; Mill believed that freedoms of thought, speech, and individuality are central to the advancement of civilization itself. However, even as one of the most ardent of libertarians, Mill did say that the government had an obligation to exercise authority over its members to "prevent harm to others," when a person's conduct "affects prejudicially the interest of others."[8]

Heretofore, the positions of Locke, Smith, and Mill as well as the opposing beliefs of Hegel and Marx were merely theoretical ideals at the time the doctrines were conceptualized. But the twentieth century provided experiments of each of these competing concepts of the ideal government. Modern libertarian thinkers were now supported by the historical record for both competitive markets and the nationalization of industry—and the next phase of libertarian thought was born.

Modern Libertarian Thought

The twentieth century produced a new wave of libertarian thought and writings, exemplified initially by F. A. Hayek and Milton Friedman, that continues to this day with Thomas Sowell. Perhaps these three can be characterized as the Socrates, Plato, and Aristotle of libertarian thought. These thinkers were not only brilliant advocates for contemporary libertarian theory but also equipped with the historical record of both large-government collectivism and small-government restraint. The works of Hayek and Friedman are so profound that to understand modern-day views on governmental restraint, each deserves individual discussion, while Sowell's prolific writings are cited throughout this book.

F. A. Hayek and The Road to Serfdom

Hayek was an Austrian-born economist who did much work in the London School of Economics as well as the University of Chicago.[9] Hayek wrote a memorandum to the director of the London School of Economics in the early 1930s in which he disputed the notion that fascism was the representation of failed capitalism. The memo then grew into a magazine article and ultimately became the 1944 book *The Road to Serfdom*. The book's first run sold out quickly, but its popularity was certainly boosted after *Reader's Digest* circulated a condensed version, which greatly increased American readership.

Hayek was particularly concerned about the support of socialism after the early twentieth-century financial problems of Europe, the Great Depression in America, and the association of Nazi Germany with capitalism. Hayek's book does a brilliant job of demonstrating the fallacies of these positions, shown later in this book, and his descriptions of the methods used to promote socialism closely resemble the edicts and actions of the modern-day left. However, those economic analyses are certainly not the thesis of this book. What are important in relation to drug and criminal justice enforcement are the principles Hayek articulates and how those principles were later related to views on enforcing criminal laws.

Hayek's Economic Positions

Hayek argued that free-market competition allowed for the adjustment of needs in society without the intervention of authority (i.e., coercive government action).[10] Furthermore, price acted as the mechanism for coordinating knowledge among the economic participants, and these positions formed the basis of Hayek's economic philosophy.[11] Hayek's work was a brilliant treatise on economic theory, but Hayek was mainly arguing for the principle of freedom. In reality, *The Road to Serfdom* was a juxtaposition between free-market capitalism (as in the democracy of the United States) and governmental economic planning (socialism), and Hayek documented and outlined how economic freedom was essential to man's overall liberty.

The Role of Government

Hayek committed much of his text to describing which government efforts are actually disastrous—namely, efforts at centralized economic planning. But he does articulate what the role of government should be in any society. Hayek believed that Europe and the United States were "moving away from the basic ideas on which Western civilization has been built."[12] He also argued against "that hodgepodge of ill-assembled and often inconsistent ideals which under the name of the Welfare State has largely replaced socialism."[13] As to the role of government in economic affairs, Hayek said society needed "an intelligently designed and continuously adjusted legal framework" to allow competition to flourish and to "prevent fraud and deception (including exploitation of ignorance)."[14]

Hayek also stated that the case for some sense of "social insurance" was quite strong, with a need in some situations to assure some minimum food and shelter for a person to be able to work.[15] However, Hayek is far from advocating for any type of welfare state; in fact, the example for this minimal insurance he articulates is a worker whose trade becomes obsolete, with the social insurance acting as a mechanism providing food and shelter, allowing the worker to survive during the transitional time over which he or she adapts to the competitive market.[16] To that end, Hayek wrote,

> Whenever communal action can mitigate disasters against which the individual can neither attempt to guard himself nor make provisions for the consequences, such communal action should undoubtedly be taken.[17]

The Rule of Law

Additionally, Hayek articulated crucial aspects that supported the foundation of free-market economics. Again, Hayek argued that any free market needs a legal framework to protect against fraudulence and duplicity.[18] Furthermore, the effective free-market society needs the "rule of law." Hayek acknowledged that the rule of law would in fact produce inequities. But, so long as the authority has not designed the law to accomplish inequity, the rule must apply to all people the same. That predictability of consistent application is crucial. Hayek used the example that it matters not whether all of society's cars drive on the left or the right, so long as they all do it the same.[19]

The Application of Morals

In his attacks on socialism, Hayek outlined the fundamental flaw in socialist thought: it

> presupposes a much more complete agreement on the relative importance on different ends than actually exists, and that, in consequence, in order to be able to plan, the planning authority must impose upon the people that detailed code of values which is lacking.[20]

Hayek believed that the "common good," the "general welfare," and the "general interest" are not sufficiently definite and that the welfare of the people in a society cannot be expressed in a single end by a government.[21] In fact, Hayek said, "The essential point is that no such complete ethical code exists."[22] Hayek pointed out that it would be impossible for any person's mind to comprehend the infinite different needs of different people, the importance of which being that they form each person's values and ethics. And when the government is left to make value judgments on who should get what, and there is no agreement among the governed, then the socialist planning authority administers what it considers to be the proper values by coercion. This, according to Hayek, is why every socialist and communist experiment has resulted in a totalitarian regime and is summarized in one of Hayek's most quoted passages: "socialism can be put into practice only by methods of which most socialists disapprove."[23]

So small-government, free-market economists do not dismiss morals, ethics, and values; like Hayek, they simply understand that the sheer impossibility of agreement on them will result in totalitarianism when such morals, ethics, and values are left to a centralized government. While Hayek certainly urged people to give to private charity and assist the downtrodden, he vehemently argued that each individual is free to make those decisions for himself or herself and that each person should bear the consequences of his or her decisions.[24] Although Hayek was generally talking about economic morality (i.e., coercive taking of property from citizens to redistribute pursuant to the values of the centralized government), this evaluation has been extended to other behaviors that can be evaluated as moral or immoral. And the application of the "morality" analysis to drug enforcement and criminal law has led many libertarians to promote drug legalization or other curtailing of law enforcement. But as we will see in subsequent chapters, criminal justice enforcement, especially narcotics enforcement, is actually crucial to libertarian orthodoxy, and we need not contest Hayek's principles on the role of government; we can in fact employ them to show the important role of narcotics and criminal justice enforcement.

Milton Friedman

In 1947, Hayek, concerned with the growing popularity of socialism, founded an international group of scholars called the Mont Perelin Society, whose goal was "to contribute to the preservation and improvement of the free society."[25] One of the founding members was University of Chicago professor Milton Friedman. Whereas Hayek's book may be the most destructive wrecking ball to socialism, Friedman's lectures and books brilliantly applied free-market principles to twentieth-century America.

Foundations of Friedman's Positions

Friedman founded his basic beliefs by citing the Golden Age of both the United States and Britain and noted that this miracle of advancement and prosperity took place during a time of little governmental participation.[26] He agreed with both Thomas Jefferson and Adam Smith that the greatest threat to the ordinary citizen is a concentrated government and that the need to protect the citizen from governmental tyranny is constant.[27]

Friedman noted the growing popularity of socialist thought among intellectuals at the turn of the twentieth century, but these beliefs resided principally with academics until the Great Depression, when these positions began to become part of U.S. government policy.[28] Friedman described Franklin Delano Roosevelt's policies as marking a "watershed" moment when the government was no longer viewed as an umpire but rather was seen as parental. This drastic change then resulted in the massive growth of the federal government that continues to this day.[29] In essence, Friedman wanted to return the federal government to the practices that produced the miracle of the Golden Age.

The Role of Government

Citing Adam Smith, Friedman articulated the limited roles of government. He outlined two of the roles as follows:

> The first two duties are clear and straightforward: the protection of individuals in the society from coercion, whether it comes from outside or from their fellow citizens. Unless there is no such protection, we are not really free to choose.

> Military and police forces are required to prevent
> coercion from without and from within.[30]

Friedman described Smith's second obligation to extend
beyond basic police functions to include rules by which
citizens can freely engage in the economic game, quite
similar to the rule of law urged by Hayek.

The third duty of government Friedman discussed is
the governmental role when two or more parties engage in
a transaction that impacts a nonparticipating party, such
as a smoke nuisance or other pollution. Friedman argued
that this role is troublesome as it can justify virtually any
government action, and the government action must also
take into account the cost of such laws. For instance, implementing any government program will require collecting
taxes, thereby negatively impacting a great number of
people for what could be a negligible impact on a much
smaller number of citizens.[31]

Friedman also believed in a fourth role of government
(although this role was not mentioned by Adam Smith): the
duty to protect members of the community who cannot be
considered "responsible" individuals. Although Friedman
cautioned that fulfilling this role of government is also
subject to abuse, he made clear, "We do not believe in
freedom for madmen or children."[32]

Friedman on Morality

Like Hayek, Friedman was very skeptical of government
authority seeking to implement morals through economic
policy (i.e., taking money from the citizenry and directing
it toward a moral cause). He cited the example of America's
social security safety net, which has been promoted as a
system good for the citizenry, whether the citizenry knows
it or not. Rather than allowing individuals to keep their
money and spend it, invest it, or save it in consideration
of their future, the government knows better than the

individual and coercively collects a significant portion of his or her income to fund and compel participation in this safety net program. Irrespective of the financial viability of this program, its advocates argue for its existence and participation on moral grounds. To that end, Friedman said, "Moral responsibility is an individual matter, not a social matter."[33] This edict from Friedman clearly impacted his views on any governmental action justified on moral grounds.

In addition, Friedman did not believe it effective when the government enforces a moral value on an individual when the individual does not share in that value. He stated,

> When the law interferes with people's pursuit of their own values, they will try to find a way around. They will evade the law, they will break the law, or they will leave the country. . . . Only fear of punishment, not a sense of justice and morality, will lead people to obey the law.[34]

And Friedman did not believe that this disrespect to the law, once born, would be limited to the specific laws with which the person does not agree. Friedman continued,

> When people start to break one set of laws, the lack of respect for the law inevitably spreads to all law, even those that everyone regards as moral and proper—laws against violence, theft, and vandalism.[35]

In the conclusion to the book Friedman wrote with his wife, *Free to Choose,* Friedman said, "Reliance on the freedom of people to control their own lives in accordance with their own values is the surest way to achieve the full potential of a great society."[36]

It is understandable how many small-government, modern libertarians have come to question both the existence and enforcement of our nation's drug laws. In fact, when viewing drug use as merely an individual moral matter, a libertarian should be opposed to drug laws (as Friedman most certainly was). But as Hayek and Friedman used both facts and the historical record to show the misunderstandings of socialism, collectivism, and centralized planning, it is now time to take the evidence we have accumulated from the historical record to demonstrate that drug laws, and the enforcement thereof, are actually crucial to the full potential of the great society that Friedman was seeking. Although many who argue in support of drug policy on the moral grounds of which Friedman libertarians are so skeptical, such arguments are not contained within this book. Rather, a closer examination of our knowledge and experience with narcotics laws, and criminal justice enforcement at large, shows that both are crucial to fulfilling the second, third, and fourth functions of government that Friedman himself supports. That is, drug distribution and drug use severely impact the internal security of our society, a person's individual use of drugs does in fact create harm to others in society, and drugs create a danger to "madmen and children" for which government must enact and enforce drug laws to protect these vulnerable individuals. Friedman himself recognized the fallibility of mankind, despite his beliefs in the utmost of limited governments as he argued that anarchy (regardless of its appeal in theory) was not feasible in a world of imperfect men.[37]

But before we further discuss the impact drug use, property crime, and the combination thereof have on our society, it is absolutely crucial to understand just whom we are talking about.

3

The Wicked among Us

Alexis de Toqueville visited America in 1831, spent nine months, and penned his observations in a very influential book titled *Democracy in America*. Among his many observations and descriptions, Toqueville noted the moral opposition to crime in the young America:

> The criminal police of the United States cannot be compared to that of France; the magistrates and public prosecutors are not numerous, and the examinations of prisoners are rapid and oral. Nevertheless in no country does crime more rarely elude punishment. The reason is, that every one conceives himself to be interested in furnishing evidence of the act committed, and in stopping the delinquent. During my stay in the United States I witnessed the spontaneous formation of committees for the pursuit and prosecution of a man who had committed a great crime in a certain county. In Europe a criminal is an unhappy being who is struggling for his life against the ministers of justice, whilst the population is merely a spectator of the conflict; in America he is looked upon as an enemy of the human race, and the whole of mankind is against him.

Clearly Toqueville's description is a far cry from the fight against criminal conduct in modern-day America. Although theories abound regarding the explanation of our nation's shift away from Toqueville's observations, a philosophic analysis as to any moral decline is not the subject of this book. This much is certain—America has significant crime. Exactly how much is caused by the drugs in our society is difficult to quantify. However, the fact that drugs do affect the crime rate (with clear and measurable evidence) is the subject of subsequent chapters.

But it would be far too general to say that America as a country has a crime problem. Crime in fact has geographical preferences—to hold otherwise would deny that high-crime areas exist. Americans know this fact very well and often choose the location of their residence in consideration of the local crime rate. Criminals exist in America—in fact, they exist by the millions.

But this truism is nothing new—deviants have existed for thousands of years, and man has recognized the evil surrounding him for just as long. Evil men were also no stranger to history's most influential thinkers. Christian Apologists found evil in all men, which came into the world through original sin in the story of Adam;[1] Machiavelli himself was dismayed at the Italian corruption of his native Italy when he wrote *The Prince*;[2] and Spinoza's teachings were based on his belief that in his natural state, a person will cheat, lie, destroy others, or engage in any other activity to help himself or herself.[3]

As illustrated earlier in outlining the seventeenth-century influences on libertarian ideals, Hobbes believed man in his original state was ferocious, whereas John Locke believed that man at his core was peaceful and sought to work with his fellow citizens. One might ask, *How could two brilliant philosophers have such differing views of the natural state of mankind*? The answer is actually quite simple—they were both correct. There are in fact men who are rooted in honesty and promote the social good while pursuing their own self-interest. But there are also men, many men, who are in fact deviants, evil, and quite unremorseful for the same. And their number and desires to victimize the innocent are vastly underestimated by both intellectuals and society at large. One cannot possibly understand the need for enforcement without understanding those whom the criminal laws are aimed to stop. As such, before we address the need for laws regarding drug use and property crime, a simple overview of habitual lawbreakers is in order.

Law Enforcement versus Intellectual Knowledge

Police officers and prosecutors deal with criminal offenders every day. Even in urban areas, officers and prosecutors are well aware of their local criminals' family history, schooling, and family dynamics. Furthermore, these law enforcement professionals have, over extended intervals of time, observed either the progressive downfall or success of these individuals. The idea that intellectuals mulling over statistics or encountering criminal deviants in a clinical setting have more knowledge, more insight, or more understanding of criminal behavior than professionals who interact and deal with these same offenders day in and day out is naive to say the least.

Law enforcement professionals have a tremendous collective knowledge of criminals. In fact, chronicling, predicting, and reacting to criminal conduct are crucial to the success of the law enforcement mission. These same professionals not only have extensive knowledge of criminal behavior but have consistently observed patterns of success and patterns of failure. When it comes to criminal deviance, police and prosecutors are a wise and savvy bunch—their success depends on applying knowledge gained through actual experience.

To be frank, a great number of the most vocal "social scientists" have oversold their ability to explain, diagnose, treat, or even cure criminal deviance. The success (or more accurately, the lack thereof) of various social science programs directed at criminal offenders is addressed in a later chapter. As it relates to the offender himself, these intellectuals simply do not fully understand these criminals; however, the law enforcement professional knows his or her adversary quite well.

If social science intellectuals had a true scientific understanding of criminals, it would be helpful if they would both assist the police in apprehending the outlaws and the prosecutors in proving their guilt once caught. However, the intellectual class has focused on promoting abstract theories on explaining deviance, usually from the perspective of mitigation of the offenses or offering some program they oversee on behalf of treating the offender. Law enforcement professionals are left to identify, pursue, deter, and deal with the actual flesh-and-blood offender in the real world. If one were to compare the historical results of the programs of the intellectual class against the efforts of the police, law enforcement would clearly have a more concrete track record of success.

That is not to say that the social sciences have completely failed to accurately describe consistent conditions of the deviant, such as a sociopath or psychopath. In fact, the utility of the work of acclaimed psychologist Dr. Robert Hare, probably the world's foremost expert on the psychopath, is also discussed in later chapters.

In addition, the practice of criminal profiling has been a useful law enforcement tool, and this discipline could be said to resemble social science. Profiling's pioneer was a Federal Bureau of Investigation (FBI) special agent named John Douglas. While working for the behavioral science unit of the FBI, Douglas interviewed a number of serial offenders. After noticing consistent patterns in the formation and motivations of the offenders, Douglas constructed criminal profiles that were successfully used not only to capture offenders but successfully in interviewing perpetrators.[4]

But Douglas, the most recognized and successful expert on violent serial offenders, never sought to explain their horrific behavior under some scientific disease model, and he has never slightly resembled an apologist for their sickening behavior. Douglas, who had studied countless violent, predatory, serial offenders, would be the first to say he had not encountered the serial offender who lacked the self-control to refrain from offending in front of police—or who did not take action to evade detection.

Laboratories and clinics have a place when applying the scientific method to human behavior (i.e., the social sciences). However, these practices have limitations—significant limitations. Social scientists interact with criminals in a controlled environment, and they are speaking with the most manipulative, morally deprived people in society. Such sterile settings use evaluation instruments that rely on self-reported information, and the self-reporters have a full understanding of the potential consequences of their answers. On the other hand, police officers and prosecutors spend their careers observing criminals in the offenders' natural environment.

To illustrate the difference in qualitative knowledge, consider the following example. A biologist could read some data regarding whitetail deer and could spend a significant amount of time observing the deer in a zoo. The data review and observations are helpful but are of very limited utility in predicting the behavior of whitetails in the wild—especially if that biologist had never even been in the woods. Now, consider a deer hunter—not just a recreational deer hunter but professional who spends each and every day in the woods, who speaks to other full-time hunters, and whose livelihood depends on his or her ability to understand the behavior of whitetail deer.

Police officers and prosecutors understand criminals—and with no disrespect to deer hunters, law enforcement professionals have a much better understanding of criminals than hunters have of whitetails. Simply propping up a position statement with academic words like "evidence-based research," "peer reviewed," or "validated" may sound good in graduate school, but it is of little meaning in the pursuit of bandits.

Fortified by decades of real experience from millions of professionals, the law enforcement community understands the reality that most habitual criminal deviants do not want a chance at a steady job or assistance from a government program teaching them "life skills." These people just elect to be outlaws. If criminals want help, it is typically when they are caught and the "help" is an alternative to punishment. Not surprisingly, individuals involved in a life of crime and rampant drug use do not contact the police or walk into a prosecutor's office and ask for help. In the execution of court-ordered wiretaps, I have listened to tens of thousands of communications between those selling drugs and those receiving the same—the number of similar text or "app" communications is even greater. These candid conversations also include discussions of the multitude of nondrug crimes used to support drug distribution and use. However, I have never—*never*—heard the communicating parties in some state of helplessness. Both regret for their conduct and any inkling of a desire to change their lives are completely absent. Although there are certainly anecdotal exceptions, these exceptions do not negate the rule. Dr. Robert Hare has noted that people in prison know very well that the word *remorse* can be very useful.[5]

The law enforcement professional is quite suspect when a phrase like *anger management* or *impulse control* is used as a quasi-scientific explanation for the criminal victimization of a citizen. Take the domestic abuser—he assaults his spouse or girlfriend, and indeed his beating is resultant from his anger. But the criminal justice system never witnesses that same individual walk up to an outlaw biker, poke the physically dominant man in the nose, and then face the ass whipping that will immediately follow. In fact, that abuser can manage his anger quite well and elects to beat the victim who cannot best the criminal in a physical altercation. It is only the fear of the negative consequences of the criminal's act that deters his acting upon the anger or impulse.

Criminal conduct and the resultant victimization act like a species in nature—perhaps more like an antibiotic-resistant bacteria: it morphs and modifies to thrive in its environment. For instance, in the early 1990s, the "good weed" sought by American marijuana users had a tetrahyrdrocannabi-nol (THC) content of 3 percent, and 1970s marijuana was estimated to have a THC content of 1–2 percent.[6] In the 1990s, marijuana almost exclusively came from Mexico or other Latin American nations. However, California legalized marijuana for medicinal purposes in 1996. As a "medical marijuana" user could not simply pick up marijuana at the corner drugstore, California also allowed individuals with a "cannabis license" to grow a certain number of plants. At that point, these individuals put significant effort into increasing the THC potency of their plants, and the THC concentration of marijuana began to increase. Today the THC content of domestic flower marijuana is over 20 percent. Incredibly, smoking one 2020 joint is the equivalent of smoking seven 1995 joints, or ten joints from the 1970s. As a result, the American domestic marijuana industry creating marijuana with such high THC content not only resulted in a mental health and public safety debacle, to be addressed in subse-quent chapters, but actually drove the Mexican cartels out of the marijuana business. The recent history with domestic marijuana production creating superweed in reaction to California's legal paradigm is but one example that can be observed throughout the United States, but this function of the learning curve among the criminal element has been witnessed firsthand by law enforcement for generations. As a foreshadowing, an analysis of our nation's recent expe-rience with the legalization of marijuana constitutes an entire subsequent chapter of this book.

As Americans leave for work each morning, take their children to school, or go out to eat, there is order in the streets. However, this order creates a false belief in the civility of many of those in one's community. Regardless of where one lives, there are rapists, child molesters, and thieves within the predatory range of one's home—there are, in fact, millions of these evil men and women in our nation, many more millions in the world, and perhaps hundreds of millions over humankind's history. If you understand nothing else about the criminal element, understand that there are men in your community who would steal every possession you have, sexually assault the women and children of your family, and victimize you in a multitude of other ways if the offender had his way. The only thing—the only thing—that prevents these predators from doing just that is a lack of opportunity or the threat of being apprehended and punished. These men do not think as you do; they are not checked by the morals that guide your conduct, and they certainly do not possess your values. Both social scientists and the public at large would be wise to heed this truism. And while their numbers may be even in the vast minority, the havoc outlaws would cause if left unchecked is incalculable.

This false sense of civility is not limited to internal strife, as the same effect can be seen in consideration of international threats. A few decades of peace among superpower nations has led many to believe that mankind has evolved from its propensity for war despite the fact that nations have engaged in warfare for as long as any form of State has existed—memories indeed fade fast. It is truly amazing that so many from recent generations maintain such faith in other adversarial nations when millions of people living in America today were alive when a Western industrialized nation attempted to take over the world and systematically exterminated more than six million Jews. But American soldiers have no such faith in our adversaries, and American law enforcement likewise does not have the naive faith in the morality of so many among us.

The writing of this book is hardly the first time I have collected my thoughts regarding the intellectual disregard for the insight of law enforcement. In fact, law enforcement is currently facing the greatest attack in my lifetime. In my frustration, I wrote an essay titled "Time to Thank the Sheepdogs," which curiously enough was written while the attacks were still new. I had no idea such attacks would continue to escalate and become platforms for social justice zealots and even presidential candidates. My thoughts on policing and the lack of respect for our law enforcement are more relevant now than when I drafted the essay in 2015, so I would like to close this chapter with those words:

Have you ever heard of Trevor Casper? Is he a household name? Trevor Casper graduated from high school four years ago and graduated from his police academy in December of 2014. On March 24, 2015, Trooper Trevor Casper was shot and killed while attempting to apprehend a robbery and murder suspect in Wisconsin. Trevor Casper was a warrior, he was a hero, and he was a sheepdog. The sheepdog metaphor is nothing new, but perhaps we should reflect upon it.

Police officers have taken a black eye recently. Much like the sins of Adam cast upon all men, a video showing an excessive use of deadly force seemingly becomes the Scarlet Letter for every police officer.

One does not have to look hard to find recent stories of high ranking political leaders falling for their corruption, or judges indicted for taking bribes. The parallel examples could include prosecutors, defense lawyers, ministers, educators, journalists, or about any profession. Yet, I do not see these rabble rousing calls for reform of the political process, education system, or even demands for increased training for those who appear in a courtroom. I do not hear Washington D.C. constantly weighing in on these sins against the public trust. Perhaps these pundits realize that the sins of the very few are not in fact all too familiar. Perhaps they believe a public official caught violating his oath shows a system at work, not a failed system.

I have had the displeasure of investigating the criminal conduct of several police officers, mostly for self-destructive behavior, but sometimes for crimes predicated upon corruption. In those extremely rare cases, the faith in my brother officers was not damaged, but made stronger. The peace officer collective has no tolerance for such conduct and the focus and effort to expose and remove it far exceeds that expressed by the typical pop culture soundbite.

We live in an era of tranquility where civilized order is the norm. For this, we should be proud. However, these cocoons of order can result in a certain naivety. In fact, so many critics have no idea of the predators among us. The ugly truth is that there are a significant number of human beings who have absolutely no morality. There are, in every community, sexual predators who refrain from abducting, raping, and molesting women and children only because of the threat of being apprehended and punished. There are even more thieves who would break into any house (even the home of a criminal apologist) to steal firearms, money, or family heirlooms if the thief knew he would get away with it.

The absence of order is not always hypothetical. Immediately after a tornado hits an urban area, there is a temporary suspension of social order, and just as quickly, looters look to steal while good people seek to help those that are hurt. The same phenomenon takes place when order is lost during a riot.

Imagine just one weekend night where every person in America knew there would be no arrests for drunk driving. Most Americans would fear leaving their homes. But tens, if not hundreds, of thousands of people would take to the road driving drunk. How many people would be killed on this one night? Yet, every weekend night, in every town, in every county, in every state, there is a peace officer working who very possibly could catch a person driving drunk and take them to jail. We all know this, we don't live in such fear, and our families are safer for it.

When the police detractors go to sleep tonight, there will be a peace officer patrolling their community. This peace officer is not just working to catch the predator after he acts, but to actually prevent the predator from hurting the detractors' families.

The most effective sheepdogs don't just catch the wolf, but keep the wolf from ever attacking in the first place. But every now and then, a wolf will attack. It is the nature of a wolf. When he does, every nearby sheepdog will take chase to catch the wolf. They will be prepared, trained, and do everything they can to catch the wolf. Sometimes the wolf gets away before the sheepdog even knows of the attack.

And a wolf that attacks once will almost certainly do it again. Only now, the wolf has learned and become more cunning, sly, and emboldened. The sheepdog is no longer a sentry, but must hunt and capture the wolf before he attacks again.

I have had co-workers—I have had friends—shot, killed, spit upon, bitten, and even stuck with a needle used by an intravenous drug user. Beyond the risk, the life of a peace officer can be hard with difficult hours, strains on the family, stress, and baseless attacks in a courtroom. Missing time with your family to investigate a crime against someone you have never met? That may sound crazy to someone who works every day in a cubicle. But I guess peace officers are different—actually, I know they are.

Almost all humans have the instinct to run from a gun fight; Trevor Casper ran to it. Sheepdogs don't run from danger. There will be peace tonight, thanks to the peace makers. Thank you, Trevor Casper. Thank you to every officer who has fallen. Let's all give thanks for the sheepdog on duty today, tonight, and hereafter.

4

Enforcement and the Small-Government Libertarian

As we have outlined and chronicled the evolution of the libertarian positions on small government, it is now time to demonstrate how the enforcement of so-called minor crimes and drug crimes (which are by no means minor) as well as a strict enforcement of the criminal justice code are imperative to achieving the objectives libertarians visualize. And to do so, we should identify exactly why so many libertarians and small-government advocates are opposed to the enforcement of our drug laws and perhaps even object to the outlawing of certain narcotics altogether.

First, we should take up the topic of a moral analysis in that Hayek and Friedman are quite opposed to governmental attempts to impose a collective morality onto those governed by the State. This is certainly where the small-government advocates place their central plank in their objection to drug laws. Even John Stuart Mill's central position was that over his mind and body, the individual is sovereign.[1]

However, both the existence and enforcement of the U.S. narcotic scheme under the Uniform Controlled Dangerous Substance Act (UCDSA) do not need to be justified on moral grounds. Although very intelligent arguments have urged enforcement of the drug laws on the moral ground of protecting the individual, such is not the subject of this book. Jeffrey B. Stamm penned an entire book on drug enforcement titled *On Dope: Drug Enforcement and the First Policeman,* which makes a persuasive case for the morality of drug laws; however, the Hayek–Friedman libertarian would clearly not be moved by any justification of the UCDSA on moral grounds.

For generations, our nation has repeatedly experienced the comparisons of drugs to alcohol bolstered by a barrage of false equivalencies between the two. To be sure, the historical opposition to individual alcohol use had been posed as a moral question, coming almost exclusively from the religious beliefs of its proponents. (The flawed comparison to Prohibition is addressed in a subsequent chapter.) This book makes no offer or attempt to persuade anyone as to the efficacy of drug laws on grounds of individual morality—with the following caveat. With regard to the moral objections to drug use, the discussion is limited solely to the personal morality of drug use, such as the users' personal self-destruction and moral objections to chemically altering the users' mood. The implications of drug use pertaining to children of users and crime committed to support the use in fact are moral imperatives for which the State has a vital role.

As we have discussed, libertarians believe every person should be left to act upon his or her moral choices. Recall that Friedman said, "Moral responsibility is an individual matter, not a social matter."[2]

But it is not simply the misplaced characterization of drug laws as solely a personal moral issue where libertarians challenge them. Any regulation of what could be characterized as private enterprise sounds the alarm for small-government advocates. The supplies and demands of drugs function as they do for any other commodity, and Hayek generally believed that a society's needs are best addressed through the free market and that, while imperfect, governmental action for some greater good results in much worse consequences.[3] Friedman loathed the role of government as parent and longed for the Golden Age, when negligible governmental restrictions resulted in the greatest era of economic and technological growth in world history.[4]

And the third leg of the libertarian antidrug enforcement stool is not limited to drug enforcement but addresses the general notion that any government program involves the expenditure of public money (i.e., the taking of people's money by coercion to fund the program). To be sure, local, state, and federal efforts to combat drugs are funded with tax dollars.

Milton Friedman appeared on the popular 1980s television show *Donahue*. Friedman was promoting his best-selling book, *Free to Choose*. In his conversation with host Phil Donahue, Friedman said the following:

DONAHUE: I assume then that if somebody wants to smoke marijuana, that is their business, too?

FRIEDMAN: That's his business, absolutely.

DONAHUE: Are we gonna take that to heroin and addictive . . .

FRIEDMAN: Absolutely. Now there, let me go back on that one because that's a very interesting thing. Even if on ethical principles, you believe it is right to prevent somebody else from smoking heroin, as a matter of expediency, it's a terrible mistake.

[I]t's a terrible mistake for society to render heroin illegal, because it increases the harm which heroin does. Why do we have so much crime in the inner cities and in the cities? Over fifty percent of it is attributed to crime for the sake of acquiring money to buy heroin. Why is heroin so expensive? Because it's illegal.[5]

This position merits analysis, but first, we must lay the foundation for small-government beliefs.

A Simple Summary of Libertarian Thought

Small-government libertarians believed that personal liberty came with economic liberty, and likewise, the loss of economic liberty led to tyranny. But although the entire premise of the movement was based on economic theory, these thinkers were not oblivious to the reality that any society has challenges beyond the basic economic system.

As we closed the last section with Friedman speaking on a talk show, perhaps we should begin this section with a subsequent appearance on the *Donahue* show. In his attempts to persuade the audience toward his positions on the role of government, Friedman put one of his basic premises in the following short summary:

> There's always a case for the government, to some extent, when what two people do affects a third party.[6]

Case closed—one needs to look no further than Friedman himself to make the case for drug laws and the enforcement thereof (i.e., government). But when it came to narcotics, Friedman was wrong—dead wrong. The disastrous impacts of increased drug use resultant from increased availability compose an entire chapter of this book. But it is worth citing one example on the heels of Friedman's quotes.

The Midwest was ravaged by methamphetamine and the resultant monumental drug and violent crime from the late 1990s until the mid-2000s. This epidemic was not the result of more expensive methamphetamine, but addicts learned how to manufacture it easily, cheaply, and purely (without the dilution of cutting agents used by drug dealers to increase quantities) from the over-the-counter cold medication pseudoephedrine. Without question, this methamphetamine crisis was caused by the widespread availability of meth at low cost due to the simplified manufacturing process, the opposite of what Friedman would have predicted.

On Christmas Day 2003, Trooper Nikky Green with the Oklahoma Highway Patrol was called to investigate a suspicious vehicle. The driver, one Rick Malone, was manufacturing and using methamphetamine in rural Cotton County, Oklahoma. Malone had recent arrests for possession of methamphetamine and manufacturing of methamphetamine. Nikky Green, a husband and father of three young daughters and a foster child, fought for his life for several minutes before he was ultimately executed by Malone. We know this gut-wrenching detail because this tragedy was captured on the dash cam of Green's patrol car. The following facts are taken from Malone's appeal of his death sentence:

¶3 In the late night hours of December 25, 2003, Appellant took his sister's car to a county road in rural Cotton County just east of Devol, Oklahoma. He set up a methamphetamine laboratory and started cook-ing methamphetamine. Appellant's four meth-making comrades, Tammy Sturdevant (Appellant's sister), Tyson Anthony (her boyfriend), James Rosser and Jamie Rosser (husband and wife) had gathered all of the ingredients necessary to make methamphetamine and loaded them in the car earlier in the day. Appellant went to complete the cook alone because Anthony became ill and stayed behind.

¶4 Before Appellant left he asked Anthony if he could borrow his 9mm pistol in case he got pulled over or had trouble with the police. Anthony understood that Appellant wanted the pistol so he could shoot and kill any officer that tried to take him to jail. Appellant had been arrested for possession of methamphetamine on November 10, 2003. On December 21, 2003, he was arrested for conspiracy to manufacture methamphet-amine. Following those arrests, Appellant explained to Anthony and his other meth-making comrades that he could not go back to jail because he would be unable to bond out. He threatened that he would shoot and kill the officers before he went back to jail.

¶5 Appellant had the lab set up on the ground outside the white four-door car. As the chemicals processed, Appellant fell asleep in the front seat. At 6:20 a.m., the local newspaper delivery person, Abigail Robles, discovered Appellant. Fearing that he was dead, Robles contacted a family friend that lived nearby. Robles traveled to Trooper Nik Green's home and woke him. Green was not scheduled to be on duty until 9:00 a.m. on that date so he reported the circumstances to the Oklahoma Highway Patrol dispatch. When Green learned that no one else was available, he volunteered to enter service early and check out the situation. Trooper Green went on duty at 6:37 a.m., and shortly thereafter he informed dispatch that he had discovered the white car.

¶6 Green's patrol unit was clearly marked as an official Oklahoma Highway Patrol car. Green pulled-up behind the white four-door car. His headlights illuminated the vehicle and the ground around the car. Apparently, Green observed the items on the ground and identified them as a meth lab.

¶7 Trooper Green was dressed in his OHP brown uniform. He contacted Appellant in the front seat of the car. Green woke Appellant by shining his flashlight and speaking to him. Green informed Appellant he was under arrest. Green had Appellant exit the car and got him face-first on the ground in front of the patrol unit. Green handcuffed Appellant's right wrist. Appellant got up and started fighting Green. Appellant later told his meth-making comrades that he fought Green because he did not want to go back to jail.

¶8 A tremendous struggle ensued on the side of the road. Green dropped his service weapon during the fight and resorted to striking Appellant with his baton. Appellant lost the pistol that Anthony had loaned him. The two men fought down into a ditch, through a barb wire fence and back again into the ditch. During the struggle Appellant found Green's service weapon laying on the ground. This gave Appellant the upper hand. Appellant put the gun to Green's head and Green stopped struggling.

¶9 Appellant forced Trooper Green to lie face down in the ditch with his arms and legs spread out wide. Appellant was on top of Green so he could not get back up. Green told Appellant that he could run and leave him if he wanted. Green explained to Appellant that he had children and pleaded with him "[i]n the name of Jesus Christ." (Tr. 5B, 975).

¶10 Appellant repeatedly asked Green where the handcuff keys were at. When Green indicated that he did not know where the key was at, Appellant explained "[t]hen you'll die." (Tr. 5B, 977). Green continued to plead for Appellant not to harm him throughout the exchange. Appellant asked Green "[w]here did you drop your gun, at?" Green pleaded "Don't shoot me." (Tr. 5b, 982). Appellant promised that he would not shoot Green. After several more requests for the keys, Green told Appellant that the keys were in his pocket. Appellant rolled Green slightly and searched his pocket. Green asked Appellant if he found the keys. When Appellant responded negatively, Green volunteered: "There's some more in my unit." Appellant stated, "I don't need to know." (Tr. 5B, 999).

¶11 Unable to find the handcuff keys or the other firearm, Appellant could not prevent the Trooper from taking further action after he left. Appellant decided to kill Trooper Green. Green recognized Appellant's thought process and began to pray. Appellant shot Green in the back of the head. Eleven seconds later, Appellant shot Green in the back of the head for the second time. Appellant cleaned up the meth lab, put the components in the car, and drove away.

¶12 Appellant drove directly to his sister's house. He told all four of his meth-making comrades: "I just

killed [*sic*] an f'ing Hi-Po." (Tr. 5B, 1021, 1037). Appellant
explained that he killed the cop to avoid going back to
jail. Appellant's comrades helped him get rid of the car,
the gun, and his clothes. Appellant apologized to each of
the four. When he noticed that Jamie Rosser was upset
the following evening, Appellant explained to her that
he had gotten everything cleaned up and that he had
left nothing to identify to him. Mrs. Rosser asked him
about the patrol car video and Appellant responded "Oh,
fuck." (Tr. 3, 143–44).[7]

Nikky Green's name is engraved on the National Law
Enforcement Memorial in Washington, D.C.; his brave
widow, Linda Green, was left to raise their children by
herself. Nikky and Linda's children are left to grow up
without the privilege of having a hero tuck them into bed,
watch their school programs, attend their ball games, or
walk them down the aisle.

Friedman simply misunderstood the drug user—living
in the world where most good people of society reside,
he had no understanding of the drug user at all. Friedman was right on the economic side of the drug trade in
that, if heroin were made fully legal, then it would become
cheaper and more widely available. However, without any
evidence or experience in drug enforcement whatsoever,
he argued that cheaper and more available heroin (or in
the previous example, methamphetamine) would reduce
the crime associated with the use of that drug. Friedman
made no mention of the increased number of innocent
people killed by the higher number of drug drivers, nor
did he say anything about the children of drug-addicted
parents. A heroin addict may "fall out" and crash, but what
of methamphetamine or PCP users, who are more violent
when under the influence. (And as is shown later in the
book, marijuana should be added to the list of drugs whose
users often turn violent.)

Friedman said that when what other people do affects

a third party, the law has a role. Mill said that as soon as a person's conduct prejudicially affects the interests of others, the State has jurisdiction over it.[8] Does outlawing methamphetamine pass Friedman's most basic test? With tears in their eyes, the family of Nikky Green would say that it does.

The Helpless and the Role of Government

The forefathers of modern libertarian thought were certainly not social Darwinists. Hayek does acknowledge that there is a case for "social insurance."[9] Now, Hayek cites an able-bodied person unable to work because his skill is no longer needed in the workplace, and he envisions that insurance as a means for food and shelter while that worker acquires a new skill to use in the workplace.[10] This is a palatable example, but a rare one indeed in modern-day American expenditures for such social insurance. Hayek, perhaps spared the disastrous consequences resulting from decades of America's welfare state, appeared not to contemplate vast populations of people who either elect not to participate in commerce as productive citizens or are wholly unable to do so because of their inability to function as productive members of society owing to drug addiction or the resulting mental illness. As outlined in the preceding chapters, Hayek and Friedman's notions that charitable needs should be fulfilled by private endeavors relate to the impoverished.

Friedman himself had a soft spot for "madmen" and "children."[11] What Friedman did not address is society's role in protecting children, protecting others from madmen, or perhaps preventing people from becoming madmen. In fact, Friedman made clear that government has a duty to protect children from their parents—even in the embryo.[12] Friedman never reconciles the duty to protect children (even in the womb) with the role of government in proscribing drug use in vitro or with the undeniable child abuse and neglect by drug-addicted parents. This is the luxury of academia. However, for those in public safety, those children and victims are not only a daily consideration; their protection is at the core of our mission.

Friedman and Hayek simply did not live in a time when we could observe how narcotics can destroy a community. They were economic theorists—revolutionary, brilliant theorists. But the application of their beliefs regarding drug addicts acting in their rational, economic self-interest has proven to be unreliable.

The harm to a child who grows up in a household marred by a drug-addicted parent is not seriously contested. It is difficult for good citizens to fathom the lack of concern drug addicts have for their offspring. Perhaps the following explanation of drug addiction from a biological perspective provides insight when viewing this phenomenon as brain chemistry rather than personal moral conviction. Our main pleasure chemical is dopamine, and it is tied to survival. If a human is thirsty and drinks, dopamine is released to receptors in the brain. The same could be said for eating or sexual activity. To further illustrate this point, it is hard to describe the care and desire a new parent feels to protect a child until one is a parent herself or himself. Some species survive by having a large number of offspring with extremely high mortality rates. Humans have but one child, yet invest considerable time in that child's protection and upbringing. In humans, dopamine release is associated with caring for a child—a biological trait promoting survival. However, many intoxicating drugs also trigger a very significant release of dopamine—and in amounts much greater than activities tied to survival. Repeated use of these drugs alters the users' dopamine distribution, and it acts like sugar in the gas tank. It is truly astonishing, and heartbreaking, to see drug-addicted parents who simply do not give a damn about their children—but they are just not wired like normal people, which illustrates the inherent shortcomings of theories that presume a drug addict behaves consistently with the general population.

This much we know—drug addicts don't maintain gainful employment, and they are not merely nonproductive citizens but commit property crime at monumental rates; their children become wards of the state, they become incarcerated, and their rampant drug use burdens the welfare rolls. Summarizing drug use as simply an individual choice with personal negative consequences is very incomplete, to say the least. There is simply no libertarian argument for legalizing drugs that acknowledges the impacts of drug use on children (nor the theft, drugged driving deaths, or violence committed by drug users against victims)—for good reason, as this reality is quite inconvenient to the libertarian objection to drug enforcement. While the casting of drug use as solely an individual choice has become the poster child of the libertarian objections to drug laws, in reality, the individual use of the drug user is a tiny fraction of what the public safety officer encounters in the streets and courtroom. The heartbreaking impacts of drug use on children and the rest of society are not theoretical but the reality in everyday America.

Ben Shapiro is a very influential libertarian in modern-day America. He has said he is "libertarian on drugs." Determining exactly what he means is not that simple. Shapiro talks about smoking "dope" and said he is "split on harder drugs" because of the addictive nature and tendency toward violence after use, that is, what he calls "externalities."[13] Shapiro has also said that he is in favor of legalizing marijuana and regulating it, making it difficult for minors to obtain, much like cigarettes and alcohol.[14] Clearly Shapiro views marijuana as a weak intoxicant associated with lethargy and "the munchies." In essence, Shapiro's statements on drugs in his lecture exemplify the entire premise of this book. Followers of Shapiro know that he constantly advocates the most important role for any individual as being a responsible parent. Clearly this book does not take issue with a single aspect of Shapiro's (or other libertarians') foundational beliefs. Rather, the simple issue is if (and how much) drug use negatively impacts others—the externalities. While Shapiro may be indifferent to legalized drug use with regard to the morality of the individual user, without a doubt, it devastatingly impacts what he characterizes as the most important aspect of mankind.

A Columbia University study found that substance abuse is a factor in at least 70 percent of all reported cases of child abuse.[15] In addition to the abuse itself, the ramifications for vulnerable children extend beyond criminal abuse. A total of 8.3 million children live in a home with a substance-dependent or substance-addicted parent—that astronomical number is greater than the combined populations of New Mexico, Mississippi, and Arkansas. These children "are also more likely to have poor physical, intellectual, social, and emotional outcomes and are at greater risk of developing substance abuse problems themselves."[16] Tragically, the abuse of children resultant from drug use often begins before birth. In the United States, a baby is born every fifteen minutes suffering from opiate withdrawal.[17] Opiate withdrawal is truly horrific—and the sterile words of the previous sentence do quite a poor job of encapsulating the impact of drug abuse on a newborn. Jeffrey Stamm described such situations, and his words bear repeating here, for one will never find such acknowledgments in the white papers of the legalization movement:

> Doctors and nurses report being able to tell which infants are going through withdrawal from out in the hallway, without even seeing them, "simply by hearing their cries." They are "hard to console" with "stiff, rigid muscles that won't relax." They have "tremors, seizures, and breathing problems and trouble feeding."[18]

Where does this fall in Hayek's social insurance? Just what is the government's role in Friedman's argument for the protection of these children? One would think the children in drug-addicted households and the opiate-addicted newborns deserve at least a passing mention when advocates analyze the impacts of legalizing drugs. Milton Friedman's protégé Thomas Sowell recognized the limits of academic and intellectual expertise. Sowell stated that intellectuals consider abstract people who live in an abstract world and that such intellectuals are not charged with putting their ideas into practice.[19] Friedman simply did not have an understanding of the drug user, as he clearly envisioned some person simply using drugs without harming others and believed more available and cheaper drugs would result in less crime supporting drug use. Even John Stewart Mill, the thinker most opposed to laws to regulate the individual, differentiated between simple drunkenness and one who drinks and impacts others: "The making himself drunk, in a person whom drunkenness excites harm to others, is a crime against others."[20]

Drug Use and Theft

Does anyone really think a methamphetamine user simply cuts down on eating out while using, or that a heroin junkie volunteers for overtime shifts (or is even actively employed) to fund his or her drug use? Copper theft, auto burglaries, and shoplifting are all driven by drug use.

Copper thefts alone cost $1 billion a year, and that is simply from insurance claims.[21] Furthermore, using 2017 data, more than 3,700 burglaries occur each and every day.[22] Approximately $13 billion worth of merchandise is shoplifted from merchants each year (about $35 million per day).[23]

The Midwest High Intensity Drug Trafficking Area (HIDTA) is composed of Iowa, Kansas, Missouri, Nebraska, North Dakota, South Dakota, and Rock Island, Illinois. In March 2020, Midwest HIDTA completed a report titled

An Examination of the Relationship between Drugs and Crime in the Midwest. The endeavor used "information gathered from modern academic research, drug market trends, substance abuse statistics, law enforcement agencies, and Midwest HIDTA law enforcement initiatives." The report found that "nearly two-thirds of the region's property and violent crime is attributable to drug use and drug trafficking."[24]

In addition, the tallies of property crime associated with drug use are vastly underreported. If one interviews any addict or his or her family, the person has stolen vast amounts of property from those closest to them, who do not report the crime. You would be hard-pressed to find a family member of a drug addict who has not gone to get family heirlooms out of pawn.

Costs

Small-government libertarians are very skeptical of any governmental program in that virtually any effort of the State must be put into place with some form of funding. The monies used to support programming come from a tax, and any tax is the confiscation of money by force. As we know, once society puts the drug laws into place, those laws are enforced by police, the offenders are dealt with in the court system, and many of them are incarcerated. All of these efforts require money, that is, the tax dollars taken by force. As such, the drug enforcement paradigm has an uphill climb in making its case to the ardent libertarian. Let's begin the ascent.

Incarceration Costs

As an initial matter, we should address the barrage of statements regarding the costs of incarceration. In criminal justice reform discussions, it would be difficult to find a false premise employed more often than the claim that each prisoner costs society a certain amount each year. As they form the basis of fiscal objections to drug enforcement, these figures deserve a closer look. In fact, how statements regarding incarceration costs are used in propaganda efforts is also discussed in chapter 5.

Promoting many bills to "ease" the state's growing prison population, Oklahoma's governor Mary Fallin stated,

> Oklahoma's prison population is well above 100 percent capacity and is projected to grow another 25 percent by 2026. The projected prison population growth could ultimately cost the state at least $1.2 billion for three new prisons and an additional $700 million in operating costs over the next decade.[25]

Any county sheriff in America would sleep well if his or her crisis were a mere 25 percent inmate growth over nine years. Public officials are quite adept at citing numbers and projections when promoting policy. Let's unpack that simple quotation. First, what is the "population"? To an ordinary citizen, that word reflects a person who is locked up behind bars—a pathetic-looking guy or gal hard on his or her luck, probably represented in a media photograph as a normal enough looking person in prison garb, helplessly gazing through iron bars with a puppy dog face. However, as this statement was made, Oklahoma prison officials were overseeing numerous "prisoners" who were simply at home wearing a Global Positioning System (GPS) monitor—who knew the term *inmate* is so malleable?

Just what exactly does *capacity* mean? *Design capacity* was a term that came into vogue among social justice advocates to argue against prison overcrowding.[26] Is capacity the total number of cots? Is it some remnant of an original design? Or is it simply the bureaucratic classification of nonmedical beds? For instance, could a correctional agency go over capacity simply by reclassifying beds under the guise of an executive decree? What is the capacity of even a three-bedroom house or a nuclear submarine?

And what of these projections? People who dedicate their careers to public safety cannot predict crime rates, crime trends, or epidemics. Where do these inflammatory projections originate? Countless formulas, time frames, and projection models could be used to forecast a number—so is this projection done for the purpose of fiscal planning or special interest advocacy?

The Vera Institute, a social justice outfit with a goal of reducing inmate populations, states that Oklahoma spends $16,497 a year on each prisoner.[27] However, the Oklahoma Department of Corrections has stated that the cost of incarcerating an inmate is $27,692 for maximum security and $14,756 for minimum security, with similar costs for a community-based prisoner. Again, one might ask, just why does it cost as much to let a prisoner go to work in the community every day and stay at a halfway house as it does to keep him or her at a minimum security prison? One might also ask where the wages for a prisoner are deposited while his or her food and lodging are provided. More importantly, what are the actual costs for a convicted inmate who is simply residing at his residence wearing an ankle monitor?

Heather MacDonald has shown that this oft-cited per-prisoner cost is an inflammatory number not reflective of reality. Contrary to the popularly quoted figure of $2,600 per month for incarcerating an individual, after the fixed costs associated with any prison, the additional cost is closer to $500 per month for each additional prisoner.[28]

The Rogers County, Oklahoma, jail is in fact its own prison. Actually, this facility faces more challenges than any Oklahoma prison in that each and every day, inmates are processed in and out. Booking, processing, and classifying often drunk and drug-influenced criminals at the height of their violence is quite unlike what happens with the static population of any prison. In fact, in a typical year, the Rogers County Jail intakes approximately 4,000 prisoners. In addition, any pretrial detention facility must in fact transport prisoners to and from court each and every day.

Furthermore, the Rogers County Jail has had wildly fluctuating inmate populations. In fact, virtually any jail in America faces a constantly shifting inmate population several times greater than that found in state and federal penal institutions. In 2011, the Rogers County Jail had a population of 180 inmates with a budget of $2.6 million. A few years later, the inmate population reached 332, with an average population of 302 prisoners. So, with this increase in jail population of approximately 120 inmates, the Rogers County Sheriff's Department spent an additional $40,000 in food and an estimated $20,000 in replacement supplies, such as blankets and jail uniforms. That increase in the jail population accounted for approximately $500 per inmate per year.[29] The preceding facts can be restated in two ways: (1) the Vera Institute's purported incarceration cost per inmate is thirty-three times higher than what it actually costs the Rogers County Jail for additional inmates or (2) the Rogers County Sheriff's Department is somehow able to incarcerate additional prisoners at about 3 percent of the incarceration cost cited by social justice advocates.

In November 2019, under the guise of criminal justice reform, Oklahoma officials oversaw the largest commutation of sentences in our nation's history. While estimates varied, as many of the commuted persons had additional sentences to serve or holds from other states, at least 450 prisoners were released in the first wave of commutations. Even by the $16,497 Vera Institute estimate, the Oklahoma Department of Corrections should be cut $7.4 million for the 450 prisoners it is no longer required to hold. This is their math, but one wonders if during budgetary requests the department will now own that per-prisoner cost that has been touted in pushing for criminal justice reform.

Enforcement Costs in Perspective—
a Comparative Analysis

Whereas to a libertarian, any governmental expenditure is significant, the enforcement costs should be kept in perspective. As we reflect on other costs, it is important to remember that both Hayek and Friedman saw the need for social insurance, and Friedman acknowledged the need for government to take a role in protecting children and madmen.

Jeffery B. Stamm penned a tremendous book advocating for the need for drug enforcement. Stamm studied the allocation of the Obama administration's drug enforcement budget and found that

> the Obama administration's total annual counter drug budget is approximately $26 billion, roughly 2.6 percent of what is allocated in one year for the continuation of Johnson's war on poverty. Of that total, fully 10.6 billion went for *non-enforcement* prevention and treatment programs.[30]

Stamm went on to determine that only $9.5 billion was allocated for domestic enforcement.[31] So, that domestic law enforcement amounts to just about 0.2 percent of the fiscal year (FY) 2020 federal budget. Furthermore, the Federal Bureau of Prisons requested $7 billion for FY 2020, which would equate to 0.15 percent of the federal budget. As public safety is one of the few undisputed roles of government, all federal drug enforcement and the entire federal prison system accounts for 0.35 percent of the federal budget. Put another way, for every $100 of the federal budget, 35 cents goes toward drug enforcement and the entire federal prison complex.

The costs of public safety funding are often cited by both the left and the right as an attack on drug enforcement. In my home state of Oklahoma, the FY 2021 legislature allocated 11 percent of the budget to public safety, which, in addition to corrections, includes multiple state law enforcement agencies and every district attorney in the state.[32] It is important to note that many local governments also get revenues from property taxes and sales tax, which are in no way part of the state's revenues. For instance, schools are funded in large part by property taxes, which form no part of the state budget and state dollars allocated to schools. As the federal government funds the military, public safety is the foremost function of state government, yet it forms a small fraction of Oklahoma's budget and is furthermore a fraction of Oklahoma's public expenditure considering all municipal and county governments.

A small-government advocate believes that any government program leads to more spending. For example, experience has shown that the increased eligibility for public assistance, disability, subsidies, Section 8 housing, or any of the multitude of government entitlement programs simply incentivized people to look for a government handout, all of which has resulted in the modern, exploded welfare state. As I will demonstrate, failure to address the drug trade (and, consequently, the related societal ills) leads to disastrous public impacts. One could say that increased law enforcement may be one of the few government program successes.

The Hidden Costs of Drugs

For some reason, public discussions surrounding public expenditures related to drug laws only include the misleading prisoner numbers and drug enforcement budgets. However, these costs are but a small fraction of the governmental costs associated with drug use and do not reflect the actual costs to private citizens. Let's again take the example of a methamphetamine lab. When individuals engage in the manufacture of methamphetamine, a number of costs are imposed on the public beyond the costs of incarceration.

The cleanup costs alone associated with the disposal of the hazardous waste can exceed thousands of dollars for one lab. Also, children living in the households of those manufacturing meth test positive in a majority of cases, so as one might deduce, the foster care and child welfare costs tied to clandestine meth labs are staggering. Furthermore, the drain on police resources from training the personnel, purchasing and maintaining protective equipment, and time dedicated to investigating conduct and processing the lab cripples the agencies. The birth of meth labs and the curious contemporary absence of illegal labs are both discussed in depth in chapter 7.

Without question, determining the total governmental costs resultant from drug abuse is difficult. Americans spend an estimated $136 billion on drugs every year (of which $32.5 billion is attributed to marijuana). Interestingly, the estimates for alcohol purchases come in at $32.2 billion.[33] Without question, the overwhelming majority of personal illegal drug use is financed by property crime, with analysis of the Midwest showing more than two-thirds of property and violent crimes resulting from drug use or trafficking.[34] Let us assume that just half of narcotics purchases are funded by property crime; then current drug use in America is funded by $68 billion in property crime committed upon Americans. That estimate assumes that a $100 theft translates into $100 in crime revenue, but in reality, the return on theft is pennies on the dollar. For instance, the wave of copper theft sweeping the nation is almost exclusively done by drug addicts. To steal a few dollars in copper at scrapyard rates requires thousands of dollars in damage to the new construction pipes, air conditioners, or power grid. Furthermore, the damage from the several car burglaries needed to fund an addict's next fix, not to mention the property loss to the victim, far eclipses the $50 for the "bump" of methamphetamine.

What about government expenditures on the massive homeless crisis sweeping America, most notably in the western states that legalized and promoted the personal use of marijuana? The crisis has been inaccurately described as a housing problem that would only be fixed with affordable housing or simple employment opportunities. But it is without question that drug abuse impacts chronic homelessness to a far greater degree than economic opportunities or the presence of public housing. The connection between the legalization of marijuana and homelessness is addressed in a subsequent chapter, but let's take San Francisco as a test case. San Francisco spends $300 million per year on the homeless—and that merely reflects the allocated budget proposal and does not reflect the drain on resources of the police, jails, public services, or the rampant theft and property damage. The *City Journal* did an analysis on the cost of the San Francisco homeless and found the city allocated more than $380 million for the homeless problem, which equated to $47,500 for each homeless person. This figure only included the budget for the city's Department of Homelessness and Supporting Housing and costs associated with health care and sanitation. The *City Journal* noted that the figure truly underrepresented the cost of the homeless population as it did not include costs accrued in the criminal justice system, from welfare payments, or from damage to infrastructure.[35]

In addition, San Francisco spent $2 billion between 2004 and 2014 for construction housing that comes with drug and alcohol counselors.[36] What positive impact did this massive budget have on San Francisco's homeless problem? The homeless population grew 17 percent in two years.[37] When hearing of a homeless individual, a good suburb-dwelling, middle-class American may envision a typical person living in his or her car simply between jobs—think again. The West Coast homeless problem is most well known for public defecation. In fact, San Francisco receives eighty calls per day reporting human feces in streets and public thoroughfares.[38] That's 29,000 poop calls per year.

The unassailable fact is that the homeless crisis is most resultant from drug addiction and ill mental health. The rise in severe mental health problems has paralleled the West Coast normalization of drugs and their increased use. This clear connection is explored in subsequent chapters, yet homelessness is but one of a multitude of hidden costs on governmental services. In fact, the costs of drug use on public expenditures are too numerous to document in this chapter. The typical drug addict does not work, steals, receives numerous entitlement benefits, and repeatedly taxes governmental services. Food stamps, welfare, SSI, disability, child protective services, foster care, Section 8 housing, and domestic violence services are just a few public services whose needs (and budgets) have soared due in large part to drug abuse. The reality is clear—drug abuse in the United States costs its citizens hundreds of billions of dollars. Furthermore, that same drug abuse leads to billions more in personal nongovernmental expenditure when considering increased costs of insurance (health and property) and actual property damage and loss. Worse yet, the cost to society grows exponentially as one includes the negative economic impact of a member of the State removed from the workforce or the loss of productivity undeniably associated with drug-addicted people. For anyone attempting to encapsulate America's drug policy simply by tallying police budgets and inflated costs of incarceration, this economic reality is a convenient omission.

However, while we have shown just a sampling of the true costs of drug abuse on government and the personal resources of our citizenry, it still remains for me to establish whether the enforcement of drug law (and conversely, the legalization and/or declination to enforce drug law) has any impact on drug use itself. Before engaging with that task, though, we should consider another type of "cost," but one that cannot be measured in dollars.

Take the case of one Neal Flowers. Flowers had approximately twenty-three felony convictions and was sentenced to eleven years in prison for drug distribution on February 28, 2016. In June 2019, the Oklahoma Bureau of Narcotics was conducting undercover purchases of drugs from Flowers. The buys took place at his home because of his "ankle monitor." That is offensive enough, but following is the text from a probable cause affidavit supporting the arrest of Flowers for actions he took while dealing drugs as a prisoner:

The victim, [Victim—name omitted], stated that on Thursday night, 6/27/19, shortly before midnight, she received a text from Neal Flowers stating that her boyfriend, [Victim's Boyfriend], had not completed a deal that he was supposed to and that he better finish it or else. [Victim] stated that she was afraid of Neal and did not want to find out what the "or else" was so she decided to finish the deal, which was to make a delivery of marijuana for Neal. When she arrived at Neal's residence at 705 N. Clayton in Wynnewood, Garvin County, she stated that she and Neal sat in a white car all night. She said that Neal had an ankle monitor from the Department of Corrections and he could not leave his residence until 7 a.m. [Victim] stated that while they sat in the car, Neal was telling her how pretty she was and that she needed to take care of him because he was taking car of her. He then took her hand and placed it on his penis and told her again that she needed to take care of him. Neal then gave her a drink which made her very sleepy. [Victim] said that the next thing she remembered was waking up in a bedroom on the floor with her shorts and panties laying beside her. She stated that she was very sore with bruising on her thighs and knew that she had been raped. When she went into the living room she saw Neal and another man whispering to each other. She then recognized the apartment and the man because she had been there before to purchase marijuana. The address of the apartment was later identified as 808

E. Williams, in Wynnewood, Garvin County, and the man was identified a Louis Larrauri. [Victim] stated that after Neal had left the apartment she told Larrauri that she needed to go but he told her that she had to wait there until Neal returned. She then told Larrauri that she needed to stretch her legs and he told her that she could go in the back yard. [Victim] looked out of a window and saw that there was a small area surrounded by a fence and she did not want to go out there. [Victim] stated she finally got the nerve to run out the front door and man [*sic*] was following her telling her that she could not leave but she just kept running. [Victim] was taken to Southwest medical Center in Oklahoma City at approximately 8:00 p.m. on 6/28/19 and examined by a SANE Nurse Robin McMurry. Her report showed that the bruising on the victim was consistent with rape.

Corey Minor was the lead prosecutor in Garvin County who sent Flowers to prison for the most recent eleven-year stint. Minor is a former army ranger who parachuted into Panama in the operation to arrest Manuel Noriega, jumping at four hundred feet to take Tocumen-Torrijos airfield—a height too low for a reserve parachute. Minor is also a former Oklahoma Highway Patrol trooper and, as a young boy, had to learn that his father, a policeman with the Norman, Oklahoma, Police Department, was killed in the line of duty. Understandably frustrated that this repeat offender was placed back into the community Minor was charged with protecting, he called the Oklahoma Department of Corrections after Flowers's rape arrest to advise them that they could initiate revocation proceedings to place him back in prison. Minor was told there was nothing to revoke—Flowers was a prisoner. The Department of Corrections website does not cite how much it costs simply to send a prisoner to his or her home on an "ankle monitor." But more importantly, we should recognize the following: some costs to criminal justice reform simply do not appear as a line item in any budget. Drug offenders commit a multitude of crimes beyond mere property crimes (which again are not "mere" to the victims). So, just how does one calculate the costs of the sexual assaults, domestic violence, child abuse, and other violence done by drug offenders? That answer is in fact simple—it cannot be done.

Drug use results in enormous costs to society. Governments spend incalculable monies on welfare, subsidized drug rehabilitation programs, mental health treatment, and foster homes, all as a direct result of drug use. While one can cite the prosecutions and convictions, these additional costs are diffused into other budgets and not viewed as costs resulting from drug availability and use. The private sector and citizens absorb tremendous increases in health insurance. The billions in theft that supports drug use are absorbed by the increased costs to all consumers. And these are financial costs—just what dollar amount should be put on the victims of impaired driving, child abuse, domestic assault, and other crimes of violence resultant from drug use? Without question, reducing drug use reduces the externalities associated with drug use—those "costs" to government, to citizens, and to the innocent.

5

Same Wolf,
Different Sheep's Clothing

If any group should be suspicious of a proposed massive structural change, created by advocacy groups and universities, and grounded on narratives perpetuated in the media, it should be the small-government libertarians. In fact, the birth and life of the criminal justice reform and drug legalization movements bear a striking resemblance to historical efforts in Western culture to advocate for expanded government programs and socialism. Whether it be the similarities in the paths that created the false narratives, the identical techniques employed to mislead the public, or even the parallel role the intellectual apparatus played in attempts to hijack the discussion, the current criminal justice reform and pro-legalization movements possess an evolution of thought and opinion (or perhaps a devolution) so closely identical to the historical and current efforts advocating socialism that the methods are more like twins than cousins. Unfortunately, in many respects, small-government libertarians fell victim to the propaganda to such an extent that they have been at the forefront of many of these movements.

Thomas Sowell opened his landmark book *Basic Economics* with the premise that it is quite easy to have good intentions but, without an understanding of how economies work, those good intentions can lead to counterproductive or even disastrous results.[1] In the same respect, as is demonstrated in this chapter, those who advocate for criminal justice reform or drug legalization clearly have little comprehension of how outlaws and drug-addicted people behave or what drives them to do what they do over and over again. Milton Friedman commented that intellectuals tend to view the state of things not as things are but as they might be—the actual versus the ideal.[2] It would certainly be wonderful if all people had the values of the intellectual class—if drug users did not commit the majority of all crimes and victimize millions of innocent people every year. The world would be a better place if ingesting high-potency marijuana impacted society no differently than drinking a beer. Intellectuals are great at ideas, but as Thomas Sowell noted in his book *Intellectuals and Society,* by viewing abstract facts through the prism of an abstract world, the intellectual class avoids the real facts in the real world,[3] has no obligation to put their ideas into practice,[4] and, worse yet, is not accountable if it is wrong.[5]

To be sure, our nation has extensive historical experience with criminal justice reform; likewise, there were sufficient facts from socialist experiments when Hayek penned *The Road to Serfdom* to enable him to effectively demolish arguments for collectivist, expansive governments. Within the book, Hayek said that we must learn from the past to avoid repeating it.[6] Yet it is not just the disastrous record of criminal justice reform from which we should learn; we must see if we recognize the methods and conditions that led to the popularization of socialist dogma and compare them to the false notions pitched to the public during these current criminal justice reform efforts.

Similar Paths, Flawed Presumptions

Hayek and Friedman spent a great deal of time unpacking socialist and big-government thought. In doing so, they diagnosed a number of flaws upon which the ideas were based. In that regard, one of Hayek's main criticisms of the viability of socialism, if not *the* main criticism, was that socialism

> presupposes a much more complete agreement on the relative importance of different ends than actually exists, and that, in consequence, in order to be able to plan, the planning authority must impose upon the people that detailed code of values which is lacking.[7]

Sowell undermined all of Marxism by attacking Marx's premise that labor is the source of all wealth, because if that were true, hard-laboring third world countries would be more prosperous than those rich in technology.[8] Libertarians challenge socialists not simply over the details but over the entire foundation of socialist philosophy, viewing socialism as a thought process built upon faulty presumptions.

In the exact same manner, each and every notion of criminal justice reform is based on a flawed presumption. Even law enforcement professionals can fall victim and make policy based on this misunderstanding. In 2017, Oklahoma decriminalized the possession of all drugs to a simple misdemeanor punishable no more than driving without a valid license. The Oklahoma Smart on Crime effort was a drastic change to Oklahoma's legal paradigm (discussed in significant depth in chapter 7), a result of which was that the district attorney's office where I worked came up with a plan to deal with this radically new legal structure. A drug investigation involves more work than the issuance of a traffic citation, such as the packaging of evidence and its submittal for laboratory testing. Even a sentence of one year in a county jail, with work credits and statutory credits, equates to just four months in jail. And once convicted, if the defendant were arrested again for the same charge, prosecutors would be unable to enhance the offender's potential sentence. Further-more, the overwhelming majority of cases are disposed of by plea bargain—the system cannot handle its volume of arrests by going to trial. But the prosecutor cannot simply recommend the maximum sentence and hope to arrive at a negotiated disposition—no rational offender accepts the maximum. The potentially more severe punishment from a trial motivates the plea agreement. As such, drug possession charges, whether methamphetamine, PCP, or the date rape drugs Rohypnol and GHB, were destined to be repeatedly pled to probation. Based on this situation, our office proposed the Drug Possession Deferral Program, known as the DPDP. This program would allow officers simply to give a citation to those found in possession of even the "hardest" of drugs and direct them to appear at the office of the district attorney's supervision division with an opportunity to get set up on a probation program with the prosecutor's office. As a conviction was practically meaningless, this program would allow persons to be placed on probation, yet a violation of this program resulted in the filing of charges rather than incarceration.

We were convinced that every drug offender would take advantage of this program, thereby avoiding arrest, any criminal charge of record, all bonding fees, and the expensive legal costs of hiring an attorney while also freeing up the criminal dockets. We set up the intake system and conducted several meetings with officers to train them on how to administer the program. Within months, the program was a monumental failure. Only a few individuals charged with possession of marijuana (and no one caught possessing other drugs) ever appeared at our office to take advantage of the program. Virtually everyone caught with drugs simply failed ever to appear and continued to use drugs, and certainly continued with the crimes supporting their drug use. Beyond our disappointment, we were very surprised—until we debriefed the initiative and drew on our experience. As we created the program, we developed it to give every incentive to the drug user to take advantage of the program—it would be completely irrational for anyone to decline to participate. But the premise on which we created the program (our own stab at criminal justice reform) was fatally flawed. We placed our values on persons using addictive, psychoactive compounds—persons who had little regard for the law or the consequences of breaking it. Whereas any career professional or soccer mom would absolutely take advantage of such a program, virtually no illicit drug users are gainfully employed, responsible parents. I have encountered a multitude of people involved in the drug world, been in their homes, listened to them on wiretaps, and read reports of what crimes they committed, and I know full well that their values are not at all similar to those of my peers. Likewise, many outlaws have simply elected to be thieves—to steal rather than work.

Such is the flaw with every criminal justice reform measure—each falsely presumes that the offenders possess the values of those advocating the policy. I doubt the reader ever thinks about beating his spouse, abusing his children, or stealing from his family, but such is the life of so many of those who have a lifestyle where they repeatedly use drugs and abandon their personal and familial responsibilities, where the rules of law are meaningless and compliance therewith is based on necessity or fear of getting caught.

Furthermore, the ideas of criminal justice reform when implemented often have similar impacts that perpetuate their existence, much like the economic meddling libertarians lament. Milton Friedman observed that big-government policies tend to be sustained as those individuals whom the policy helps are visible, but those who are hurt by the policy are anonymous.[9] In that same vein, criminal justice reform measures are typically associated with a person who is released—that inmate may even form the basis of a political campaign commercial. However, an inmate released from prison is arrested on average five times within nine years of release, with 44 percent getting arrested in the first year. And if someone were to claim that a drug offender is simply arrested for a new drug offense, more than three-quarters (77 percent) of released drug offenders are arrested for a nondrug crime within nine years of release.[10] Even the preceding statistic is sanitized, as is illustrated with a specific example described in chapter 7 (of the heroin addict who completely evaded detection for years despite stealing several times a week to support his opioid habit). Put simply, it is actually difficult to get caught—in fact, getting caught is oftentimes a random event and a function of the law of large numbers based on the frequency with which outlaws habitually break the law. Consequently, the violence, copper thefts, shoplifting, child neglect, and additional devastation wrought by drug offenders and other criminals are completely invisible to the public debate, and the common citizen does not associate drug use with events categorized as other crimes.

Milton Friedman did a marvelous job discussing the challenges and misconceptions of big-government policies in twentieth-century America throughout his lectures and writings. Friedman was especially critical of special interest groups—once any law is passed, a special interest group is created, even if it is the bureaucracy that implements the law. And once created, the special interest group is quite adept at maintaining its lifeblood—government funds. To be sure, the policy debate regarding criminal justice reform is markedly similar when discussing budget implications.

Friedman categorized the competing interests as concentrated versus diffused interests. He used the example of federal subsidies of the merchant marine industry, which came in at $600 million. Friedman calculated that that $600 million equated to $15,000 for the individuals involved in the industry but only $3 for each American taxpayer.[11] As such, those concentrated few had an enormous interest in the continued funding, while it was unnoticeable to each taxpayer. Friedman noted the same effect in the industries lobbying for tariffs,[12] agricultural subsidies, or even the operation of the U.S. Postal Service.[13]

When it comes to criminal justice reform, especially among those pushing for decriminalization from a budgetary perspective, the basic premise is that decriminalizing certain conduct or legalizing drugs will reduce incarceration, which reduces government expenditures for prisons. A significant portion of a subsequent chapter will demonstrate that the costs and purported savings of releasing criminals are markedly false and propagandized, but these "savings" at least represent a number on paper. The costs of having these offenders back in society are simply ignored and, like the taxpayer supporting the merchant marine industry, are invisible and diffused through society at large.

Sowell spent much of his career advocating against the disastrous effects of minimum wage laws. He commented that it would be comforting if the government could simply decree higher wages for all without having to worry about the unfortunate repercussions.[14] Likewise, everyone, especially public safety professionals, would be quite content if society could indiscriminately release its drug and property offenders from prison without these people victimizing children, innocent victims, or society at large. Certainly such a utopian result is what every advocate for criminal justice would want, but Sowell also prefaced his treatise on economics with the truism that life presents us, not with what we want, but rather with options[15]—and weakening criminal laws and releasing offenders offer no panacea but carry serious consequences. In Britain, the total cost of incarceration was determined to be under £2 billion, but the cost of crime committed by criminals in the country was estimated at £60 billion.[16] The devastation wrought by drug users is repeatedly discussed throughout this book, and the same will not be rehashed here. But this much is absolutely clear—any presentation by a decriminalization or drug legalization advocate simply points to a purported savings in incarceration costs without any discussion of the effects of their platform (i.e., Sowell's unfortunate repercussions). This glaring omission is by design or perhaps arises from patent ignorance, but if the public were truly aware of the impacts of such programs, their support for such initiatives would become negligible.

In 2010, the Cato Institute, an esteemed conservative think tank, published a paper by Harvard University lecturer Jeffrey Mixon and doctoral candidate Katherine Waldock that forecasted substantial economic savings to the United States if our society were to fully legalize drugs.[17] Put simply, the authors took the estimated cost of enforcing the drug laws while also adding up the tax revenues associated with legal sales. That seems simple enough—but math premised on false presumptions is still flawed math. This naive view of drug use has been addressed throughout this book, but it bears repeating, as this uninformed view composes the entire basis for the reform movements. Here are just a few important omissions in the essay:

1. The paper takes no account of the fact that the overwhelming majority of drug use is funded by other crimes committed upon society (such as theft or robbery).
1. The paper does not address, even in passing, the violent crimes committed by those under the influence of narcotics (violent assaults, stabbings, shootings, rapes, etc.).
2. The paper presumes that use rates will be static after legalization.
3. Combining numbers 1, 2, and 3, the paper does not account for the increased use and resultant increased crime visited upon the innocent.
4. The analysis takes no consideration of the impact drug abuse has on other government services, such as child protective services, homeless programs, publicly funded drug treatment programs, or virtually any entitlement.
5. The paper makes no mention of the impact substance abuse has on nongovernmental costs, such as increased

premiums for health insurance, car insurance, and theft insurance.

6. The collateral damage to the nation's children could be the subject of a book in and of itself. Perhaps the thousands of infants born each year experiencing severe opiate withdrawal from maternal prenatal drug use merit at least a footnote.

One should not be overly impressed with the Ivy League credentials or academic degrees of those postulating these abstract notions. Hayek himself noted that those thinkers whose work paved the way for totalitarian regimes were sincere in their ideals while also being men of "considerable intellectual distinction."[18]

In the same way socialism has been promoted based on false assumptions, the current criminal justice reform movements are based on faulty premises—advocates for criminal justice reform incorrectly assume that habitual offenders possess the values and mores of responsible citizens. Public safety professionals, perhaps both unburdened with servitude to abstract theory and rich in experience, know this very well. Without question, police officers and prosecutors are ardently opposed to these reforms not because of ideology or political affiliation but based on their complete understanding of the criminal deviant.

Same Techniques: The Nobility of the Cause

It is obvious that the playbook the left used to promote socialist and big-government ideas also was used to push society toward false notions that supported criminal justice reform—both movements were cloaked in the nobility of the cause. Hayek outlined in *The Road to Serfdom* the genesis of thought supporting the turn-of-the-century intellectual movement toward socialism, as the coercive government policies were promoted under the guise of social justice.[19] Friedman noticed that all of the movements for expanded government policies were done in the name of welfare and equality.[20] Sowell has observed that movements among the intellectual class are typically characterized by the values of "caring" and "compassion,"[21] and words such as *caring, compassion,* and *social justice* are undefined, malleable in the hands of those with "verbal virtuosity."[22] Whether they be for marijuana legalization or the release of prisoners, criminal justice reform movements always operate under the guise of compassion. Step 1: complete.

Same Techniques: The Perpetuation of Myths

Once the noble cause is established, the next step is to create a myth to justify the proposed action. Hayek noted that socialist planners would construct assertions and create associations between what was desired for the socialist objective and such assertions.[23] The modern-day big-government interventionist policies are based on myths of designed racial or sexual discrimination in virtually every aspect of Western culture (loan applications, employment, student discipline, college admissions, etc.). These myths have been debunked by other writings, and such is not the topic of this book. What is important is the following: the government policies libertarians so deride are premised on such myths—perpetuated by the intellectual–special interest–media complex. Criminal justice reform is likewise premised on a multitude of myths. Here are a few:

1. Minorities are incarcerated at higher rates than whites for identical crimes.
2. Prisons are filled with persons charged with only the possession of drugs.
3. First-time drug possession and property offenders are sentenced to incarceration.

4. Minorities are shot by police at a higher rate than whites for like encounters with police.
5. Marijuana is not addictive, has been shown scientifically to have medicinal properties, has no association with violence, is an alternative to opioids, and has no impact on cognitive abilities.
6. Marijuana legalization is a binary choice between legalization and pediatric seizures and opiate addiction.
7. Criminal justice reform will result in massive savings from a reduction in the prison population.
8. The taxing of legalized psychoactive drugs will be a boon to public coffers.

Same Techniques: Pseudoscience

Once the motivation is established, the myths are engrained and repeated, and the next step for the apparatus is the application of pseudoscience. Hayek devoted a significant number of pages in his book to documenting the repeated attempts to extend the scientific renaissance toward society. Much postwar socialist thought was born of a cult of science by Fabian Socialists.[24] In fact, Hayek observed that the intellectual class engaged in the crude application of scientific ideals to society.[25] As such, the false notion that a scientist can direct and control societies' economics like a chemical reaction in a lab was responsible for the intel lectual class and universities concocting pseudoscientific principles.[26] Put simply, Hayek observed that we simply cannot master the forces of society as scientists had learned to master the forces of nature.[27]

Anyone who has been even a tangential student of socialist growth and big-government thought should recognize the methods used to promote many criminal justice reform measures. Terms like *evidence based* and *validated* used in conjunction with some evaluation instrument that is supposedly predictive of future deviance are commonplace in today's criminal justice system. However, virtually every public safety officer knows that the best predictor of future behavior is past conduct—put more simply, those who commit crime and use drugs usually continue to commit crime and use drugs. The application of Hayek's criticism of science to society differs little from the purported application of science to human deviance.

To be sure, the discipline of psychology has been of great help to criminal justice professionals. Robert D. Hare wrote a book titled *Without Conscience: The Disturbing World of Psychopaths among Us*. It is my opinion that Dr. Hare's book should be required reading for every career police officer and prosecutor. In the end, Hare finds that psychopaths are, well, extremely disturbed and that society needs to be protected from such people. Hare's book does a tremendous job identifying what constitutes a psychopath, and the absolute utility of the book lies in its basic simplicity and recitation of facts. Yet Hare's tremendous and useful book did not come into my hands from social scientists seeking to assist enforcement; rather, it was a gift from a prosecutor and close friend named Isaac Shields. Isaac was a psychology doctoral candidate who was deployed into combat as a military officer during his graduate studies. He is a tremendous prosecutor, and law enforcement is quite fortunate Isaac changed career paths after returning from combat. It was Isaac's early study of psychology and psychopathy that allowed him to realize the utility of Hare's work for public safety professionals and prompted him to share the book with other prosecutors.

Sowell has noted that in psychology and literature, the exceptional theory is regarded as important, quite unlike among doctors, who are exceptional because of their adherence to accepted professional standards.[28] In much the same way, social scientists typically proffer a solution to the human conditions of deviance, a defect existent for tens of millennia, and the criminal justice world has now clearly been impacted with Hayek's pseudoscience, Friedman's special interest, and Sowell's intelligentsia.

The Apparatus

Once the pseudoscientific creed Hayek described is formed, then the apparatus adheres to the creed[29]—the cult of science Hayek observed with Fabian Socialists.[30] Hayek made a point to say that this movement was perpetuated by sincere idealists of intellectual distinction.[31] Hayek described it as follows:

> And the whole apparatus for spreading knowledge—the schools and the press, radio, motion picture—will be used exclusively to spread these views which, whether true or false, will strengthen the belief in the rightness of the decisions taken by the authority; and all the information that might cause doubt or hesitation will be withheld.[32]

The political and social leanings of the American "mainstream media" complex are certainly no secret. Bernard Goldberg wrote an entire book on predispositions and prejudices of the media, titled *Bias*. Goldberg, a former CBS insider, was blackballed for exposing the bias in a Wall Street Journal op-ed. Goldberg's book certainly identified the partisan political bias. For instance, ABC, NBC, CBS, and CNN ran seventy-one homeless stories during G. H. W. Bush's four years in office, ostensibly caused by Reagan, but only nine such stories over Clinton's entire eight years in office. Furthermore, Goldberg noted that the media will typically identify a party to a story as conservative or "right-wing," but there is no such labeling of liberals or "left-wing" individuals or organizations.[33]

Beyond the "partisan" bias, Goldberg also chronicled an absolute bias for cultural issues. During the Reagan administration, the media completely parroted the home-less numbers put forth by the homeless lobby, which were exponentially higher than the known homeless population, thereby creating a false notion of a homeless epidemic in the 1980s.[34] Goldberg also chronicled the media complex presenting the 1980s AIDS epidemic as a heterosexual threat while refusing to show the high number of infections from intravenous drug use. The federal government spent millions on an "AIDS does not discriminate" campaign, and one about which Oprah Winfrey said in 1987,

> AIDS has both sexes running scared. Research stud-ies now project that one in five—listen to me, hard to believe—one in five heterosexuals could be dead from AIDS at the end of the next three years. That's by 1990. One in five. It is no longer just a gay disease. Believe me.[35]

While Goldberg brilliantly outlined the reporting ineq-uities during his career, the bias of the modern-day media culture is much worse. The divide between media values and the values of the general public is certainly greater now than it was when Goldberg wrote his book. And the pop culture media's position on drug laws, incarceration, and criminal justice reform fell into lockstep with the intelligentsia apparatus.

To a great extent, this is described in chapter 6, regard-ing the propaganda related to marijuana. But Alex Beren-son made an interesting observation in his book *Tell Your Children the Truth about Marijuana, Mental Illness, and Violence*. Berenson would be the first to say that as a Yale-educated former *New York Times* reporter, he was attacked by his colleagues when he dared to write a book documenting the mental illness and violence associated with cannabis use. In fact, Berenson believes that the marijuana movement itself represents an abject failure on the part of the North American media establishment in promoting the positions of the legalization lobby without acknowledging the established science undermining the entire movement. In that regard, Berenson spends a great deal of his book discussing the work of Dr. Robin Murray of the United Kingdom. Dr. Murray is arguably the most prominent schizophrenia researcher in the entirety of Europe—and he has little doubt as to the association between marijuana use and increased schizophrenia.[36] Furthermore, Berenson cites a collection of European mental health professionals and an editorial in the *British Medical Journal* discussing studies in Sweden, Holland, and New Zealand (one study alone has been cited 1,300 times) that stated,

> Although the number of studies is small, these findings strengthen the argument that cannabis increases the risk of schizophrenia and depression, and they provide little support for the belief that the association between marijuana use and mental health problems is largely due to self-medication.[37]

The facts, notions, and evidence Berenson cites in the book are not unknown in Europe. In fact, Europe is not facing a massive marketing campaign at every level of the apparatus, similar to North America's current experience, and not surprisingly, the use rates of marijuana in Europe are falling at a time when such rates are skyrocketing in the United States and Canada. Berenson attributes this to what he calls the "transatlantic knowledge gap."[38] Perhaps Western culture across the Atlantic has learned from tolerant penalties for drug offenses as, contrary to the current North American trends, Europe has been steadily moving toward increasing penalties for drug offenses.[39]

This phenomenon is not unique to drug legalization and criminal justice reform. In *Intellectuals and Society,* Sowell outlined how reporters are part of the apparatus, as they filter and slant facts in accordance with the prevailing views of the intelligentsia,[40] and that nonprofit "experts" are absolutely riddled with agendas and bias.[41] Friedman, when he wrote his book *Free to Choose* in 1980, noted that the universities, media, and bureaucracy compose the "new class" and had become an especially powerful special interest.[42]

As of the writing of this book in early 2021, one still hears stories in which an "expert" advocating for marijuana legalization relays a personal anecdote claiming that cannabis cured his or her cancer—and these are not hyperbole or exaggeration but actual stories appearing in the media in which a person claims that ingesting a mood-altering carcinogen cured cancer. As if this were not bad enough, the media does not challenge the claims, much less interview an oncologist to seek out any evidence that the stoners found the cure to cancer, which has eluded modern medicine for generations. Without question, the criminal justice reform movements have received an assist from the media complex, as has been done with many of the notions birthed by the intellectual left.

Propaganda

Hayek described the propaganda employed by the "apparatus" when promoting socialist ideas, in that when the sources of information become uniform, the minds of society are quite easily molded to beliefs consistent with the propagandists' ideals.[43] In its efforts to accomplish this, Hayek noticed that the propaganda effort gave new meaning to old words.[44] Likewise, the criminal justice reform movement redefined a multitude of words. For instance, as outlined in chapter 6, marijuana itself was rebranded as medicine, and the term *medical marijuana* is commonplace in modern-day America. Stealing and other property crimes are now often referred to as "crimes of poverty." Even the term *low-level crime* is a malleable term encompassing many violent offenses no reasonable person would consider "low level." Yet these phrases are used in founding the premise upon which many criminal justice reform measures are based. The word *incarceration* itself, which has historically meant one who is imprisoned behind bars, can now include persons on a GPS ankle monitor at home. While the public at large envisions the prison population to be those behind the walls of a prison, a government agency can simply declare that someone at home wearing an ankle monitor is an inmate.

Prison overcrowding is typically premised on the number of inmates over "capacity." It would be difficult enough to determine the capacity of a three-bedroom house, much less a multiprison complex, yet a correctional agency has carte blanche to define its capacity. For instance, first suppose a correctional agency defined its capacity simply as nonmedical beds. At any point, a government official could simply reclassify beds from standard beds to medical beds; as a result, without a single person entering or leaving the prison system, the prison is by "definition" over capacity through simple wordsmithing. If you think such games are not played, think again.

Sowell has noted that intellectuals engage in "verbal cleansing" to make the proposed policies appear more palatable. For instance, a swamp is renamed "wetland," a prostitute is called a "sex worker," and even self-identified labels morph from progressive to liberal and back to progressive.[45] Sowell has long advocated for the questioning of statistics put forth by governmental and advocacy groups. In a speech in the 1990s, Sowell outlined his effort to unpack the statement regarding how many people in this nation were hungry—decades later, there are still billboards and policy made based on this notion of millions of hungry people suffering in America. Sowell, after noticing that a special interest group had stated how many Americans were hungry, wondered how hundreds of millions of Americans were surveyed to determine who was hungry. In examining the methodology, Sowell discovered the group took census data, determined how many people were eligible for food stamps, then took the number of persons getting food stamps, subtracted those obtaining food stamps from those that were eligible, and presto, all of those people who remained were "hungry." Using this method, the advocacy group determined the hungriest county in America, which turned out to be a farming community where the employees and employers ate what they grew. As a result, the monetary income of these individuals would be smaller while also removing any need for food stamps. With hunger, reality was much different than the conclusions posited from statistics. While claiming millions of poor Americans were not eating, Sowell noted that there was no evidence that poor children are more clinically underweight compared to the more affluent, nor do blood samples show evidence of protein or vitamin deficiencies greater in poor people compared to other income brackets, with one exception—low-income women do have a slighter tendency to obese, as Sowell quippingly notes, presumably because they must be very hungry.[46]

Steve Lewis served as the speaker of the Oklahoma House of Representatives, is currently a Tulsa lawyer, and "represents clients at the Capitol." In May 2019, Lewis wrote an opinion piece advocating for the drastic reduction in Oklahoma's prison population. His basic premise was that if Oklahoma reduced its prison population rate to the national average, the state would save more than $164 million per year. Lewis writes, "It's not asking too much that we at least strive to be average."[47] The logic seems compelling—until one looks at the numbers underlying Lewis's position.

While Oklahoma claims that it spends $16,497 per prisoner, here are some statistics from other states on the cost per prisoner: Massachusetts, $55,170; Rhode Island, $58,564; New Jersey, $61,603; California, $64,642; and finally, New York, $69,355—a whopping four times more than is spent in Oklahoma. In fact, the national average spent by states is $33,274, more than twice the figure cited for Oklahoma. Only two states list incarceration costs cheaper than Oklahoma: Alabama at $1,717 less than Oklahoma and Louisiana at $246 less per prisoner a year.[48] I wonder if Mr. Lewis and the criminal justice reform fiscal hawks wish to strive to spend at least as much per prisoner as the national average. In fact, if Oklahoma simply had the national average incarceration rate with the national average for cost per prisoner, the state would pay $140 million more on incarceration. If these numbers approached reality (again, the fraud of incarceration costs is addressed throughout this book), then every correctional director would seek to learn just how Oklahoma could imprison offenders so cheaply—the Oklahoma Department of Corrections would be a beacon of fiscal light for the small-government libertarian. However, the numbers are not reality but a function of how each state defines inmates and incarceration. In Oklahoma, an "inmate" includes a convict on preparole release, at a halfway house, or an offender sitting in his or her own home on a GPS monitor. Oklahoma can incarcerate so cheaply in part because correctional officials have elected to define inmates and incarceration in a certain way.

As I was writing this book, I had pulled several numbers regarding the costs of incarceration from the Oklahoma Department of Corrections website in December 2019. Later, in February 2020, I went back to the website to get the numbers for a colleague who was participating in a debate on prison overcrowding, but the numbers were thousands of dollars higher per inmate compared to the figures posted just two months prior. Oklahoma was in the process of reducing its prison population based on a number of measures during various reform movements. As costs of incarceration are simply created by taking the overall budget divided by the number of inmates, the cost of incarceration per inmate will increase when the prison population decreases without a corresponding reduction in budget. Incredibly, by releasing inmates under the pretense of saving incarceration costs, Oklahoma instantly calculated an increased cost to house an inmate. One should wonder why a fiscal conservative would place so much faith in government accounting.

In *The Road to Serfdom,* Hayek noted how advocates for socialist ideas would effectively sway the docile and gullible with vague ideas that were imperfectly framed.[49] In the same fashion, these criminal justice reform and drug legalization movements are little more than sound bites and memes directed toward good, God-fearing citizens in such a way as to appear palatable, but they are utterly ridiculous to those who deal with public safety each and every day.

Other Similarities

Beyond the striking similarities between the advocacy of socialist-type big government and criminal justice reform outlined already in this chapter, many likenesses remain that deserve mentioning. First, Friedman commented that radical ideas are often financed by a few wealthy individuals.[50] Modern-day criminal justice reform and legalization efforts have benefited greatly from their benefactor, billionaire George Soros. Soros gave $100 million to the Drug Policy Alliance,[51] an organization dedicated to the complete decriminalization of "responsible drug use." National Families in Action (NFIA) conducted research regarding the marijuana ballot initiatives titled *Tracking the Money That's Legalizing Marijuana and Why It Matters.* NFIA found that contributions from three billionaires constituted such a significant portion of the monies supporting these efforts that the paper's opening reads,

> We place contributors who support marijuana ballot initiatives into one of several categories. The Three Billionaires category contains contributions made by George Soros and/or Peter Lewis and/or John Sperling and the marijuana legalization organizations the first

two fund themselves (Soros) or through their families (Lewis, who died in 2013).

The paper's findings are alarming across the board. For instance, in California's 2016 Proposition 64, which legalized recreational marijuana, the Three Billionaires category accounted for $22,829,841 in money raised to promote the passage, which was out of $38,179,439 in total money raised for both sides. In fact, of that total amount, $35,667,001 was raised to promote the passage for recreational marijuana, compared to $2,512,438 raised to oppose recreational marijuana. That is, 93.4 percent of the money spent in California's legalization initiative was in support of legalization. The disparate impact of the Three Billionaires' contributions toward legalization is not unique to California, nor are the out-of-state special interest contributors seen supporting other criminal justice reform initiatives.

But who is to oppose these efforts? The best-situated and most-informed individuals would be public safety professionals—but police officers and prosecutors are a mission-driven group who are committed to the daily grind of protecting the public. These people simply do not hire lobbyists or raise money for public messaging, and the information from public safety officials was limited to periodic media interviews—hardly a counter to a professional (an extremely misleading) marketing campaign. So, one must ask, has the American value system on the legalization of drugs and criminal justice reform really changed, or has this well-organized decriminalization campaign simply utilized the same socialist and big-government propaganda techniques that libertarians so despise?

Friedman noted that every society in history is somewhat dissatisfied with the distribution of income, and that dissatisfaction is exploited by advocates of radical ideas.[52] In modern-day America, a growing dissatisfaction with the costs associated with imprisoning those who break the law has been utilized by those proposing the historically failed ideas of decriminalization and "reform."

The most striking parallel between socialist ideas and criminal justice reform proposals is that the purported beneficiaries of each are actually those who are hurt the most. For instance, minimum wage laws are supposedly designed to help those lowest on the wage ladder. Yet time and time again, those hurt most by such laws (through the reduction in such employment, which has been documented each and every time) are the lowest wage earners because so many of them will no longer have any income at all.[53] Friedman made a similar claim with regard to public housing programs, as such efforts were made to benefit the poor but ended up hurting lower-income individuals with the creation of compressed living and slums.[54] Likewise, as I have documented throughout this book, the proxies of each criminal justice reform movement are the most negatively impacted. For instance, the lack of enforcement makes poor, oftentimes minority neighborhoods much more dangerous than the gated communities of the elite. The legalization and decriminalization of drugs actually lead to greater drug use, higher rates of addiction, and personal devastation for users based on the much higher use rates that follow legalization. Furthermore, crimes motivated by drug use take place predominantly in these struggling neighborhoods (see chapter 7). And sadder yet, as demonstrated in chapter 6, the parents of epileptic children were promised miraculous benefits from the administration of cannabis to these developing brains, and while the parents were victims of the propaganda machine deployed on the American public, the children were victims of the drug use itself.

Conclusion

Conservatives long ago identified the propaganda techniques to promote disastrous big-government economic policies, among other leftist causes. We would all be wise to greet these promotional activities that advocate for curtailing enforcement with the same skepticism, as it's not just some of the same people promoting these ideas but an implementation of an identical playbook.

6

The Experience of Legalizing Marijuana

Our nation has recently experienced the legalization of marijuana for recreational and even "medicinal" purposes. In a way, these legalization efforts are a microcosm of every thesis within this book. From the pro-legalization propaganda to the devastating impacts on the communities that legalized marijuana, the small-government advocate can learn much from these experiments in decriminalizing marijuana. To be sure, it would be hard to imagine a greater fraud placed upon the American public than the successful recasting of marijuana from a psychoactive street drug to a safe and effective medicine. Amazingly, this was done by promoting a scientific model abandoned in the 1700s and supplemented by age-old, yet familiar, propaganda techniques.

The Fraud of "Medicinal" Marijuana: The Background on the UCDSA and FDA

Throughout our nation's history, we have had certain concepts that were once accepted by the general public but later seemed ludicrous—typically such misconceptions are promoted by an interest group that benefits from the deceit. The trifecta of this generation's debunked notions inevitably will be *Cigarettes don't cause cancer*; *Opioid pain medication is not addictive*; and *Marijuana is medicinal*.

The Uniform Controlled Dangerous Substance Act (UCDSA) is the basic legal scheme for the drug laws in the United States. It is "uniform" in that the basic framework has been passed federally and in each of the states. The UCDSA operates as follows: The universe has an infinite number of compounds (substances), ranging from water to complex chemical formulas. However, some substances are recognized to be very dangerous, and as a result, these compounds are controlled by law.

Once a substance is controlled, the UCDSA outlines five schedules, with Schedule I being legislatively recognized as the most dangerous and Schedule V as the least dangerous. In fact, Schedule I substances are not recognized as having any legitimate medical purpose. The typical Schedule I substances are drugs such as heroin, gamma-hydroxybutyric acid (the date rape drug GHB), and phencyclidine (PCP), and until a 1996 ballot initiative in California, marijuana was a Schedule I drug—legislatively found to have no valid medical purpose by every single state and the U.S. Congress.

Schedules II through V are subject to potential abuse, but the use of these substances is overseen by practitioners (i.e., physicians), administered by a professional in the lawful course of his or her practice (i.e., use of an anesthesia during surgery), delivered by a licensed dispenser (i.e., pharmacy), or even possessed by a private person pursuant to an order from a practitioner (i.e., a prescription). The UCDSA provides for all of the lawful possessions, uses, and deliveries for these substances under the clear rules of the act.

Within the realm of medicine, the United States utilizes the Food and Drug Administration (FDA) to determine whether a substance is safe before it is marketed to the public. In 1937, an American business promoted a substance called elixir sulfanilamide to heal everything from a sore throat to a sexually transmitted disease. But when more than one hundred Americans died after taking the elixir, including thirty-four children, the United States experienced a national scandal and took steps to prevent it from happening again. The Elixir Tragedy of 1937 resulted in the FDA playing a vital role in determining the safety of so-called medicines prior to saturating our nation with such compounds.[1]

Now, simply proclaiming that a substance has medicinal properties is a bit incomplete in light of modern science. For one thing, scientists look at the dose–response relationship of any medication. If the dose is too small, then the medication will not work, and if the dose is too large, it may do more harm than good.[2]

Furthermore, consideration of side effects from any medication is crucial in determining the efficacy of a substance and establishing an FDA-approved use for it. For instance, intravenously injecting morphine is sure to cause the user a dopamine-induced euphoria. However, no physician treating a patient for depression would recommend mainlining (injecting) morphine to treat the depression, due to the risk of overdose, the potential for abuse, and the likelihood of addiction. Consider even alcohol—our nation has a well-known history of medicinal use of alcohol as an anesthetic for surgery (i.e., the use of alcohol on Civil War battle-wounded soldiers prior to performing a surgical amputation). However, no modern-day anesthesiologist would consider giving a patient a few shots of bourbon prior to a knee replacement, despite the medicinal potential. It would take far too great of a dose of alcohol to get the response needed for rendering someone unconscious for a major surgery—the risk of such a large dose would be tremendous, and most importantly, many other medications currently work much better.

The most well-known compound in marijuana is tetrahydrocannabinol (THC). However, THC is a Schedule III substance known under the pharmaceutical brand name

Marinol. Marinol can be prescribed for nausea and even some treatment of narcolepsy. Marinol is a tablet containing a mere 2.5 milligrams of THC. However, the THC content in marijuana varies, and it is impossible to accurately calculate the THC intake from smoking marijuana. One would not ask a pharmacist how much vitamin C is in a children's chewable vitamin and receive a response akin to "100–200 milligrams, depending on the quality and skill of the manufacturer." Yet that is all a "bud tender" at a medical dispensary could offer a customer when describing the THC contained in the flower marijuana. Whether for controlled drugs or over-the-counter medications, FDA guidelines require dosages to be replicated in perpetuity so that the user knows exactly what quantity is being ingested and to guard against accidental overdosing.

Marijuana's other compound with purported medical benefits (which at present are still under FDA trials) is cannabidiol (CBD). CBD is extracted from the marijuana plant and has no psychoactive properties, but CBD has been removed from the definition of marijuana, so CBD is as legal as aspirin—just less regulated. Following these legislative amendments to the definition of marijuana, CBD shops began to pop up across the United States. It is this author's prediction that CBD will go the way of magnetic bracelets and wonder juice made with berries from the tropical rain forest—health fads born from silly marketing with a short shelf life.

The Campaign for Medical Marijuana

Much like the snake oil salesman of the nineteenth century as well as the promises preceding the Elixir Tragedy, proponents of so-called medical marijuana have said that marijuana alleviates virtually any ailment. However, two purported medical justifications served as the virtual front men of the medical marijuana movement—the treatment of epilepsy in children and a safer alternative to the opiate crisis crippling America.

Childhood Epilepsy

More than two thousand years ago, Aristotle outlined three methods of persuasion—*ethos* (ethics), *pathos* (sympathy), and *logos* (logic). Aristotle's approach is still taught to advanced legal practitioners to this very day. When it came to medical marijuana, its advocates clearly chose sympathy as the method of persuasion and fully abandoned logic. The effort was marked by a media barrage of parents who pled for the legalization of marijuana to alleviate the seizures in their children. Whether it was an opinion piece written by a mother saying her young child was not a stoner or a broadcast media story with footage of a darling child whose parent spoke of her little one's horrendous seizure and the need for legalized marijuana, the issue was presented to the public as a binary choice between legalized marijuana and continued seizures of these afflicted children. If it would "help" a child, how could anyone with a heart or an ounce of sense object to full medical legalization?

In essence, the entire promotion of medical marijuana for pediatric epilepsy was done by the presentation of anecdotes—and not from the medical community but from the parents who had watched their children suffer, praying for anything to make it better. In the latter part of the 1700s, Western culture was swept by the practice of harnessing animal magnetism to cure a host of ailments, a notion created by Austrian physician Franz Mesmer. As the reports of cures grew, Mesmer began to train disciples, who would harness the animal magnetism to cure patients—for a fee, of course. Both the Mesmerizers and the patients were reporting clear and positive results from the practice. But none other than Benjamin Franklin, American ambassador to France, was asked by the French to test these claims. To do so, he and a team of scientists utilized "blinded" studies.

When Franklin and his colleagues applied the blind method to the application of animal magnetism, they found it was not effective at all—despite the sincere anecdotes claiming it worked.[3] In modern-day practice, researchers in a double-blind study administer a placebo along with the tested medical substance to the sample groups. Neither the researcher nor the patient knows who gets the placebo and who gets the actual medication—hence, it is doubly blind. Franklin and company discovered that when testing a theory, there is natural, and very strong, tendency for both the tester and the patient to observe and/or feel positive results. This tendency is not nefarious but a reflection of natural human hope.

Since our nation's infancy, we have known better than to practice medicine or conduct scientific inquiry by anecdote. And in modern-day America, support for the use of marijuana for the treatment of epilepsy in children is on par with the use of animal magnetism by a Mesmerizer to treat the ailments of the 1700s.

While the sole method used to persuade the public of the positive effect of marijuana on epileptic children was *pathos* (sympathy), the absence of *logos* (logic) and facts was even more offensive. The public debate was not a debate at all—only the "enlightened," counterculture hipsters had a platform, as the medical experts and specialists were absolutely absent from the discussion. Perhaps we should quote Dr. Michael D. Privitera, MD, president of the American Epilepsy Society—it is highly unlikely you heard from him in any media exposé when the American public was informed on the issue of medical marijuana:

> The American Epilepsy Society has been opposed to the expanded use of medical marijuana, and its derivative, cannabidiol or CBD, in the treatment of children with severe epilepsy. At this time there is no evidence from controlled trials that strongly support the use of marijuana for treatment in epilepsy. Our position is informed

by the lack of available research and supported by the position statements from the American Academy of Neurology, the American Academy of Pediatrics, and the American Medical Association.

At present, the epilepsy community does not know if marijuana is safe and effective treatment nor do we know the long-term effects that marijuana will have on learning, memory, and behavior, especially in infants and young children.

An observational study by a team from Children's Hospital Colorado that was published in the April 2015 issue of the journal *Epilepsy & Behavior* found that artisanal "high CBD" oils resulted in no significant reduction in seizures in the majority of patients and in those for whom the parents reported improvements, these improvements were not associated with improvement in electroencephalograms (EEG's), the gold standard monitoring test for people with epilepsy.

Additionally, in 13% of cases reviewed seizures worsened with the use of cannabis and some patients there were significant adverse events. These are not the stories that you have likely heard in your public hearings or have read in popular press, but they are the reality of AES members who are practitioners at Children's Hospital Colorado who cared for the largest number of cases of children with epilepsy treated with cannabis in the U.S.

As a result, the epilepsy specialists in Colorado have been at the bedside of children having severe dystonic reactions and other movement disorders, developmental regressing, intractable vomiting and worsening seizures that can be so severe they have to put the child into a coma to get the seizures to stop.[4]

Opposition to the use of medical marijuana in children does not come simply from police or prosecutors, and the most fervent objections did not come from teetotaling evangelicals on moral grounds. Rather, very intelligent, committed scientists who get up every day to help children experiencing seizures were not merely agnostic on medical marijuana for children with epilepsy but vehemently opposed to it. In consideration of the medical experts, it appears that the association between cannabis and the reduction of pediatric seizures is actually weaker than the eighteenth-century claims of the Mezmerizers. Sometimes informed facts are inconvenient to narratives striving for validation. Why let some solid *logos* undermine the *pathos*? Anecdotal sympathy is one helluva way to conduct science.

An Alternative to Opioids

Rahm Emanuel once opined that a policy maker should not let a crisis go to waste.[5] Employing Emanuel's edict, medical marijuana advocates, with an assist from the pop culture media, promoted marijuana to solve the most looming drug crisis seen in decades, perhaps ever—the opiate epidemic. Beginning around the 2016 presidential election cycle, public officials appeared to have just come to realize that opioid pain medication is addictive. This was not a secret to anyone who worked in law enforcement or drug treatment during the preceding decades, but in 2016, the addictive nature of opiates became a topic of public discourse. The United States contains a little over 4 percent of the world's population but consumes 99 percent of the hydrocodone in the world.[6] If one were to attribute higher drug consumption to the better medical infrastructure, unfortunately, America's life expectancy ranks lowest among comparable countries.[7] Unless one thinks millions of people are walking around Japan, China, Europe, or India in intractable pain, America has a problem with opiate consumption. As one might expect, America also has a severe opiate overdose problem. In 1999, the United States had 16,849 fatal drug overdoses. As the totals steadily increased with a clear upward trend starting in 2008, by 2017, our nation buried 70,237 citizens for fatal drug overdoses, with legally manufactured and dispensed pain medication being responsible for the historic increase.[8]

With that backdrop, the promotion of medicinal marijuana was littered with stories indicating that it is a safer alternative to opiate pain medication. This was curious indeed, with all the research pointing to marijuana as a "gateway drug."[9] But why misrepresent *logos* without a dash of *pathos*? Thus the media story was never simply about presenting an opinion; perhaps the story would portray a young combat veteran who claimed to be taking more than twenty pain medication tablets a day and who pleaded for the legalization of medicinal marijuana so he would not have to take so many. Again, the public was presented with a false binary—between legalized medicinal marijuana and the pervasive use of opiate pain medication. When tested against a placebo, marijuana as a pain reliever is akin to Advil or Tylenol.[10] As Alex Berenson observed, much like alcohol, marijuana is an intoxicant first and a painkiller second.[11]

It should be noted that there is an association between marijuana use and opiate use—but it is the opposite of what was presented to the public. In fact, if a person uses marijuana, his or her risk of opioid use disorder increases threefold. If the person is a heavy marijuana smoker, then the risk is eight times greater.[12] Initial *JAMA* research received a great deal of media attention when it appeared to show that opiate overdoses were lower in states that legalized marijuana.[13] But the updated data did not receive as much media attention. In 2018, a study published in *JAMA* found that

> the opioid crisis appears to be worsening in states where marijuana was legalized, despite fewer opioid prescriptions, and as such constitutes evidence for the gateway hypothesis and against the marijuana protection hypothesis.

In 2019, *JAMA* updated the opioid study and found that "medical marijuana was associated with a 23% increase in opioid deaths." Furthermore, an editorial in the professional journal *Addiction* found that the proposition that legalized marijuana availability stops opiate overdoses to be "weak."[14] While the rates of overdose deaths were lower in states with legalized marijuana until 2010, Alex Berenson looked at the data and showed that the initial variance in overdoses was a function of geography. The opiate epidemic started in the Midwest, while marijuana legalization began on the West Coast, so as the opiate epidemic spread nationwide, the legalization states had an accelerated rate of overdose.[15] If only facts and science got as much airtime as sympathetic anecdotes.

But the negative association between marijuana and pain medication was not limited merely to fatal overdoses—a *Lancet* study found that people who used cannabis had greater pain and lower self-efficacy in managing pain with no evidence cannabis use reduced pain interference or exerted an "opioid-sparing" effect.[16] In fact, in 2018, researchers for *Patient Safety in Surgery* found that patients reporting marijuana use actually experienced more pain on average when admitted to the hospital following traumatic injury than those who did not, and compared to nonusers, they required more opioid medication to cope with pain and consistently rated their pain higher during the duration of their stay.[17]

If any organization should have an informed opinion on the availability of marijuana as a counterbalance to addiction, it should be the American Society of Addiction Medicine (ASAM). In fact, it has unequivocally been on record since 2012 regarding marijuana's impact on drug abuse. On July 25, 2012, ASAM's board of directors adopted the "White Paper on State-Level Proposals to Legalize Marijuana." Here are some highlights:

ASAM has a well-earned and long-established reputation of approaching drug policy issues from its unique position as the leading organization of physicians and experts in addiction with knowledge of the risks associated with the use of substance with high abuse potential.

ASAM opposed proposals to legalize marijuana anywhere in the United States, including the current state-based legalization proposals which will appear on November 2012 ballots.

ASAM asserts that the anticipated public health costs of marijuana legalization are significant and are not sufficiently appreciated by the general public or by public policy makers. Physicians and other health professionals must become more aware of the anticipated undesirable outcomes of marijuana legalization and encourage public education on these facts.

Marijuana as a gateway drug is not seriously contested by experts.[18] Tragically and deceitfully, communities reeling from the devastation caused by a "medication" promoted as safe and nonaddictive were told that widespread availability of marijuana would be a panacea to our nationwide abuse of opiate pain medication. Only science, experience, and history told a different story—and the worst is yet to come.

Addictive Nature

As an initial note, there is a misconception regarding marijuana that is as pervasive as it is inaccurate—that marijuana is not addictive. While Barak Obama is not a member of the media per se, he is certainly part of the pop culture complex that sought to normalize marijuana. The fight against protecting our nation from the dangers of cannabis was certainly not made easier when the leader of the free world used his bully pulpit to claim marijuana use was simply a "bad habit and vice, not very different from the cigarettes I smoked as a young person up through a big chunk of my adult life." Obama absolutely did not make America safer when he said "I don't think [marijuana] is more dangerous than alcohol."[19] For a man who berates anyone who questions global warming models as "deniers," Obama certainly has the ability to ignore science when it fits his narrative.

What say the experts about marijuana and its addictive qualities? The proposition that marijuana is addictive and harmful is endorsed by the World Health Organization, the National Academy of Sciences, the National Institutes of Health (NIH), the American Society of Addiction Medicine, the American Medical Association, the U.S. Surgeon General, the American Academy of Pediatrics, and the American Academy of Child Adolescent Psychiatry, to name a few.[20] But these educated and professional positions get little, if any, coverage compared to some pundit claiming that marijuana is neither addictive nor harmful.

Potency

As we have discussed, the psychoactive (and dangerous) compound in marijuana is THC. In the 1970s, the THC content of marijuana was between 1 and 2 percent.[21] Furthermore, burning marijuana in a joint or pipe destroys about half of the THC.[22] In the mid-1990s, the THC content of marijuana (imported almost exclusively from our southern border) was approximately 3 percent. But in 1996, California legalized marijuana for "medicinal" purposes. A pot user could not run to the corner drugstore to fill his marijuana prescription, so California authorized the medical marijuana recipients to grow a certain number of marijuana plants.[23] Consequently, marijuana growers focused intensely on breeding, cloning, and producing marijuana plants with extremely high THC content. Beginning in the late 1990s, the potency of marijuana coming into the Drug Enforcement Administration testing labs steadily increased in THC content, and today the THC content of flower marijuana is over 20 percent.[24] Beginning in about 2010, two types of marijuana were on the street in nonlegalized states: reggie (regular marijuana from Mexico) and high grade or kush (marijuana typically grown on the West Coast or possibly in Colorado). At present, reggie is virtually nonexistent—in fact, under the personal medical paradigm of the West Coast and the small personal use laws of Colorado, the resultant black market supplied the entire nation with highly potent marijuana such that cartel marijuana was no longer in demand due to its weak THC content.

One may applaud moving the black market marijuana business into America from Mexico, but providing the ability for drug traffickers to produce the marijuana domestically carries a hefty price tag. If one were to smoke a joint today, thanks to American industriousness, smoking that joint would be the equivalent of smoking seven joints from 1995 and more than ten joints from the 1970s. What's worse, California weed advocates promoted THC extraction methods to harness pure THC to be placed into candies or other edibles or simply ingested in pure form, called "dabbing." The widespread availability and dramatically increased potency of marijuana would prove to have disastrous consequences for the communities that allowed it.

Mental Health Impacts of Marijuana Use

The association between a multitude of mental health ailments and marijuana use is so profound that only the greenest of the Green the Vote marijuana advocates deny the connection—and many of them even concede that marijuana accelerates mental illness.[25] However, this association is simply dismissed as the mentally ill self-medicating. But researchers studied nearly fourteen thousand Australian twin pairs drawn from 1992 to 2009. More than six thousand of the twin pairs were monozygotic (identical twins), with the remaining sample size being fraternal twins. As identical twins have the same DNA, the study would account for genetic predisposition, and as fraternal twins were studied, any claim that correlations were due to environmental factors and upbringing would be observed for twins born at the same time and simultaneously raised in the same household. The findings were shocking—frequent users of marijuana were nearly twice as likely to develop major depression compared to the identical twin who did not, and suicidal ideation was 2.47 times greater in the identical twin who frequently used marijuana. Put more simply, "the study suggests a causal relationship between frequent cannabis use and both major depression and suicidal ideation."[26]

Perhaps we should look to the National Academy of Sciences, Engineering, and Medicine for its take on the dangers of marijuana. The academy was chartered in 1863 by Congress to advise the nation on issues of science. The academy currently comprises approximately 6,300 scientists, who volunteer to seek objective, scientifically balanced answers to difficult questions facing the nation.[27] The National Academy of Sciences alone has approximately 2,350 members, of which 190 have received Nobel Prizes.[28] The National Academy drafted a report in January 2017 titled *The Health Effects of Cannabis and Cannabinoids,* which had the following findings:

- For individuals diagnosed with bipolar disorders, near daily cannabis use may be linked to greater symptoms of bipolar disorder than nonusers.
- Heavy cannabis users are more likely to report thoughts of suicide than nonusers.
- Regular cannabis use is likely to increase the risk for developing social anxiety disorder.[29]

Regarding other mental illness, the report also stated that "cannabis use does not appear to increase the likelihood of developing depression, anxiety, and posttraumatic stress disorder."[30] However, one would think the academy would update this finding relating to depression, as nine months after its report was published, the clear association between marijuana and depression was shown by the extensive study of identical and fraternal twins, as discussed earlier.

But the most important mental health finding of the academy's report did not deal with social anxiety, depression, or bipolar disorder. In fact, the single largest collection of Nobel Prize–winning scientists the world has ever seen reported on the connection between marijuana use and disassociations from reality. The report's lead finding on marijuana and mental health read as follows:

- Cannabis use is likely to increase the risk of developing schizophrenia and other psychoses; the higher the use the greater the risk.[31]

The West Coast of the United States is currently experiencing a severe and growing homeless problem—and it has everything to do with the decriminalization of drugs and scaling back of law enforcement. Unable to blame the problem on capitalist policies during a booming economy and record low unemployment, the homeless problem was first described as a "housing crisis." But the current state of California, Washington, and Oregon homelessness is not your garden variety homeless problem. The West Coast homeless problem is represented first and foremost by discarded drug syringes, mountainous trash generation, and even homeless people defecating on the sidewalk. Ultimately, the media accurately encapsulated the current homeless problem as a crisis resultant from severe psychosis and drug addiction, but no one asked why the West Coast had an exploding population of drug addicts and severely mentally ill people (with much overlap between the two).

Let's review what we've outlined in this chapter so far:

1. In the late 1990s, the West Coast legalized marijuana, and both the use rates and potency of marijuana increased.

Smoking a West Coast joint in 2020 is the equivalent of smoking seven 1995 joints and more than ten 1970s joints.

2. A panel of the largest concentration of Nobel Prize–winning scientists unequivocally concluded that marijuana use increases the risk of schizophrenia and psychoses—the higher the use, the greater the risk.

3. Virtually all scientific experts have concluded that marijuana use greatly increases the occurrence of other substance abuse disorders.

4. During a thriving economy, the West Coast experienced a visible and crisis-level increase in homelessness characterized by severe psychosis and drug addiction.

It is maddening that no one seems even to slightly ponder what has caused this increase in severe psychosis and drug addiction. Is it plausible that scores of people were taking a dump in the street for generations completely unnoticed, or that public defecation was as much a part of the 1980s as the Cold War, acid-washed jeans, and break dancing? Or is it more likely that the levels of drug addiction and psychosis have recently dramatically increased due to some new external cause? The science of epidemiology tells us that *If X causes Y, then more X causes more Y.*[32] To plug our facts into the formula, *If marijuana use causes drug addiction and psychosis, then more marijuana use causes more drug addiction and psychosis.* We are not talking rocket science but simple pattern recognition that epitomizes the intelligence of mankind. The most primitive animal either stops doing things that cause harm, or the animal is destined to extinction. A dose of primal intelligence just may do our nation some good.

Marijuana and Violence

With the clear association between marijuana and psychosis, the next issue relates to the impact the increase in severe mental health problems has on societal violence. As mentioned in an earlier chapter, Alex Berenson, a former reporter for the *New York Times,* wrote a tremendously compelling book on the violence that results from legalizing marijuana: *Tell Your Children the Truth about Marijuana, Mental Illness, and Violence.* Berenson was inspired to write the book after conversations with his psychiatrist wife, who noticed the continual association between marijuana smoking and the mentally ill in her practice. Berenson chronicles the history of marijuana not just within the United States but throughout the world. Berenson's book is an absolute must-read for anyone who has any interest in the implications of legalized marijuana. Berenson's thesis and support thereof are absolutely compelling, and among a trove of other data, he cites the following academic studies relating to the association between cannabis use and violence:

- The correlation of marijuana use to violence is greater than that of alcohol.[33]
- Each of the four states that legalized marijuana saw an increase in aggravated assaults and murder after legalization.[34]
- A 2012 paper found that the use of marijuana doubled the risk of committed domestic violence.[35]
- People with psychosis are five times more likely to be violent.[36]
- A 2012 study of twelve thousand high school students found that marijuana smokers were three times more likely to be violent.[37]
- A study published in the *American Journal of Psychiatry* found that of 278 people charged with homicide (excluding vehicular homicides), over 32 percent had been diagnosed with cannabis dependence or abuse (compared to 23 percent with alcohol dependence or abuse).[38]
- A 2016 paper in *Psychological Medicine* documented a long-term study that showed that marijuana users had a nine-fold increase in violent behavior, which was even higher when accounting for other variables.[39]

- In 2000, a study published in the *Archives of General Psychiatry* found that people with marijuana dependence are at four times the risk for violence.[40]

It should be of no surprise that the increased incidence of mental illness among marijuana users is not limited to the self-destruction of the user but also is enacted in violence upon our citizenry.

Marijuana and Intelligence

The NIH is a federal agency dedicated to research in biomedicine and public health.[41] The NIH is composed of twenty-seven separate institutions and centers from various scientific disciplines. In 2019, the NIH was ranked second in the world for biomedical sciences by *Nature Index* when measured by the largest contributors to papers published in leading journals from the preceding four years.[42] One of the NIH's institutes is the National Institute on Drug Abuse.

In August 2013, the National Institute of Drug Abuse published findings from a twenty-five-year study on marijuana use and cognitive abilities. The study found that regular marijuana use (more than four days a week) beginning before age eighteen is associated with an average Intelligence Quotient (IQ) decline of 8 points by age thirty-eight.[43] That 8 points of IQ loss amounts to falling from the 50th percentile to the 29th percentile.

The NIH study found that memory, processing speed, executive function, verbal skills, and attention (i.e., virtually every kind of brain function) were all measurably reduced.[44] And the loss in intelligence was not detected only by the testing instruments; the loss of cognitive ability in the marijuana smoker was quite apparent to those individuals close to the smoker. Worse yet, researchers found that the impact on cognitive ability was drastically worse for adolescent, developing brains.[45]

Did it really take twenty-five years and a peer-reviewed scientific study to tell America that high school stoners are stupid? To be sure, the study was crucial in that finally we scientifically quantified the debilitating effects marijuana use has on mental function. But it was not scientists, evangelicals, or law enforcement who first promoted the notion that weed smokers are idiots—that has always been their shtick. Cheech and Chong, Jeff Spicoli, and even a movie titled *Dazed and Confused* all recognized the dumbassery of a pothead.

The Outlook

But it's time to look at the glass half empty. The NIH study on marijuana use and IQ went back twenty-five years; the National Academy of Sciences looked at data going back decades; the studies of Australian twins may have been released recently, but the information relating to mental health diagnoses pertained to marijuana use several years prior; and finally, all of the data showing marijuana as a gateway drug were years in the making. What should be terrifying is that the test subjects for the preceding scientific findings were ingesting at most 3 percent THC marijuana, while today's growing number of marijuana users are consuming marijuana with THC concentrations 700 percent higher.

The Experiments with Legalization

The legalization debate relating to all controlled dangerous substances, especially in libertarian thought, is rooted in theory, with each of the respective policy advocates founding his or her arguments based on his or her different view of the world. However, we no longer need to discuss abstract theory; we now have several years of data on the effects legalized marijuana has had on the communities that allowed it—data that can be compared to states that kept marijuana illegal. As we will see, not a single prediction of those advocating for legalized marijuana came to pass—in fact, the results were the complete opposite of what was promised.

Use Rates

Advocates of legalization of drugs will often proclaim that drugs are like the forbidden fruit in the Garden of Eden—that rules prohibiting their consumption actually lead to greater use. And without exception, any argument or analysis promoting the legalization of drugs presumes that use rates will at most be static once the drug is legalized. The notion that outlawing the distribution and consumption of any drug has no impact on the rate of that drug's distribution and use defies common sense. But again, those arguments are based in validating beliefs about human nature, and those beliefs have been decimated by the evidence. For instance, in 2005, approximately 3 million Americans engaged in daily use of marijuana, but by 2019, that number has nearly tripled to 8 million.[46] The American Society of Addictive Medicine has explained that once a substance is legalized, the perceived threat is reduced, thereby leading to increases in use.[47] Furthermore, once marijuana was legalized, profit seekers clearly engaged in the promotion of marijuana use. This can be illustrated by the following statistics: in 2017, Denver had 392 Starbucks establishments and 208 McDonalds but 491 marijuana stores.[48] Marijuana traffickers in a legalized market needed a larger number of marijuana users. Unfortunately, they succeeded.

Let's first look at the youth use rates and begin with Colorado. The Rocky Mountain High Intensity Drug Trafficking Area (RMHIDTA) conducted an extensive report analyzing a multitude of evidence in Colorado both before and after legalization. Throughout these reflections on Colorado, it is important to note the following time frames:

- The years 2006–8 comprised the precommercialization era.
- The years 2009 to present comprise the medical marijuana and commercialization and expansion era.
- The years 2013 to present comprise the recreational marijuana era.

The report found that Colorado's youth ranked number 1 in the nation for past-month marijuana use in 2014–15 and had ranked number 14 just nine years prior. In fact, in the three years prior to 2014–15, youth use rates climbed 12 percent, making Colorado's youth use rate 55 percent higher than the national average. That could be a coincidence—there are fifty states in the union, so there is a 2 percent chance of a coincidental anomaly. As we have illustrated the association of marijuana use with suicide, in a tragic correlation, in the years prior to commercialization, known toxicology for suicides for Colorado residents 10–19 years old showed 13.5 percent testing positive for marijuana. In the 2009–12 commercialization era, that rate rose to 17.4 percent, while alcohol toxicology rates for suicides among this age group declined.[49] Similarly, the "normalization" of marijuana in Holland was followed by a threefold increase in youth use rates.[50] Beyond Colorado, the states with the top ten youth use rates are legalization states, while the ten states with the lowest youth use rates have no legalized marijuana.[51] The chances that the correlation of both higher child marijuana use in legalized states and lower child marijuana use in states that have outlawed marijuana is simply coincidental would approach the odds of winning the lottery. The principle of Ockham's razor holds that the simplest solution is usually the correct one—one wonders what tortured analysis a legalization advocate would use to explain the preceding disastrous relationship between legalization and child marijuana use.

The rate of marijuana use for college-aged residents in Colorado increased 16 percent in the three-year average between 2013 and 2015, which puts that rate 61 percent higher than the national average.[52] Other than drug dealers, it would be hard to find anyone who would be pleased with such an increase in marijuana consumption among college students and children. But the greatest increase in marijuana use was among Colorado adults. In fact, the three-year average in "past-month" marijuana use among adults in Colorado between 2013 and 2015 increased 71 percent from the average of the preceding three years. This increase moved Colorado from the seventh ranked state to the number 1 state for adult marijuana use, with an adult marijuana use rate 124 percent higher than the national average. In the three years prior to 2013–15, Colorado's marijuana use rate was a mere 51 percent over the national average.[53]

Similarly, Oregon, which commercialized recreational marijuana in July 2015, saw daily cannabis use rates jump from 29 percent to 37 percent between 2014 and 2015.[54] In fact, a whopping 28 percent of cannabis users reported more frequent use after legalization.[55]

The state of Washington, which had also legalized marijuana in 2012, saw increases as well, albeit not as dramatic as Colorado. Regarding use among children age twelve to seventeen, Washington's marijuana use rate increased 3.18 percent from 2011 to 2014.[56] These increases in children using marijuana are concerning enough standing alone but are even more dramatic when considering that during the same time period, the national average of the twelve- to seventeen-year-old marijuana use rate *dropped* 2.21 percent.[57] In fact, a peer-reviewed study regarding the impact of legalization efforts found that "nationwide, overall use rates in states that have legalized marijuana outstrip those that have not."[58]

Adverse Reactions, Hospitalizations,
and Treatment Admissions

As the use rates for children and adults increased dramatically, it is important to determine if many of the adversities associated with marijuana use also increased. In 2011, Colorado reported 6,305 hospitalizations related to marijuana. By 2014, that number had increased to 11,439. From January to September 2015 (the latest data available from the RMHIDTA's report), the number was already at 11,901, on pace for more than 14,500 annual hospitalizations.

Marijuana-related exposures (poison control calls) in Colorado increased 139 percent for the four-year average (2013–16) compared to the four-year average prior to legalization,[59] and marijuana-only exposures increased over 210 percent. Most alarmingly, poison control calls regarding exposure to marijuana among children more than tripled after legalization, and 42 percent of the exposed children were age zero to five.[60] During the same respective time periods, poison control calls for adults more than quadrupled.[61]

With all of this, it is no surprise that Colorado averages well over six thousand treatment admissions into drug treatment programs for marijuana each year, more than for methamphetamine, and more than twice as many as the treatment admissions for heroin.[62] In 2007, 22 percent of people in all drug treatment in Colorado reported using marijuana heavily. With steadily increasing rates, by 2014, that number had jumped to 36 percent reporting heavy marijuana use.[63] For anyone concerned about the actual cost of marijuana legalization, it would be pure nonsense to think these increased poison control calls, hospitalizations, and drug treatment admissions have no impact on public expenditures, medical costs, and insurance rates. In fact, one Colorado hospital alone experienced $210 million in uncollected payments from marijuana-related admissions,[64] and states that legalized marijuana saw a 10 percent increase in automobile insurance premiums the year of legalization and a 16 percent increase the year after legalization.[65]

In Oregon, researchers found that "between October 2015 and October 2016 [recreational marijuana was commercialized in July of 2015], the rate of cannabis-related diagnostic codes in emergency department visits rose 85 percent."[66] The data further showed that "marijuana-related calls to [Oregon poison control] increased exponentially from 2014 through 2016."[67] In fact, between 2014 and 2016, calls to Oregon poison control related to marijuana increased 337 percent.[68]

Drugged Driving

It is clear that once Colorado legalized the use of marijuana, consumption of marijuana measurably increased at every age demographic, which was reflected in dramatic increases in hospitalizations, emergency room visits, and poison control calls. Considering that marijuana is the most common drug involved in drugged driving,[69] it should not be surprising that the states that legalized marijuana experienced dramatic increases in marijuana-impaired driving. An Oregon study found that 21–34 percent of marijuana users drive within three hours of use.[70] In the state of Washington, 8.8 percent of drivers involved in fatality accidents tested positive for marijuana in 2012. Yet after legalization, each year, the percentage of positive tests was significantly higher, and by 2017, 21.4 percent of drivers involved in fatality accidents tested positive for marijuana—an increase of 243 percent.[71] The impact marijuana use has on driving can be summarized by the National Institute on Drug Abuse, which stated, "Marijuana significantly impairs judgement, motor coordination, and reaction time. Studies have found a direct relationship between blood THC concentrations and impaired driving ability."[72]

Research by the Governors Highway Safety Association found that states with legalized recreational marijuana experienced a 16 percent increase in pedestrian fatalities during the first six months of 2017, while all other states experienced a 5.8 percent decrease.[73] In the four years after legalization, Colorado experienced a 66 percent increase in marijuana-related traffic deaths compared to the preceding four years.[74] In 2009, the percentage of drivers involved in fatality accidents testing positive for marijuana was 9 percent. By 2016, that percentage had more than doubled to 21 percent. Put another way, in Colorado, drugged driving went from killing roughly one person every six and a half days to killing a person roughly every two and a half days after legalization was passed.[75] It seems callous indeed merely to represent these victims of drugged driving in a bar graph showing the substantial increase in people killed by marijuana-impaired drivers—while the goal here is to present the facts unimpeded by sympathy, it must be remembered that each of these deaths was a devastating blow to the loved ones of the person killed. But to make matters more concerning, the staggering increase in marijuana-related impairment is clearly underrepresented in the statistics. The RMHIDTA report contained this alarming paragraph:

> Colorado now mandates that traffic fatalities within the state be analyzed to see what role drugs played in the crashes. State police are re-analyzing samples from suspected drunk drivers in 2015 and a Denver Post source stated, "more than three in five also tested positive for active THC." However, testing remains expensive and most departments stop testing when a driver tests positive for alcohol impairment.[76]

Impact on Crime

Many who advocate for the legalization of any drug are concerned about the individuals who are themselves charged with drug crimes. So, the argument goes, by decriminalizing marijuana, there should be a sharp reduction in marijuana arrests and prosecutions. Although the percentage of persons incarcerated for marijuana use is estimated at only 0.5 percent, with the vast majority of those individuals actually involved in distribution,[77] mari-juana legalization is continually promoted as having the potential to curb incarceration costs.

With respect to children in Colorado, the number of juveniles arrested for marijuana-related offenses increased 5 percent from 2012 (prior to legalization) to 2014 (post-legalization).[78] In what should be alarming to any social justice warrior, the percentage of white juveniles arrested for such offenses went down 8 percent, while arrests of Hispanic juveniles went up 29 percent and the arrest of Black juveniles increased 58 percent.[79]

Denver had eight citations for the unlawful public display or consumption of marijuana in 2012. By 2015, that number had exploded to 752.[80] In Boulder, there were seventy-two citations in 2013 for the public consumption of marijuana; by 2015, that number had more than doubled to 151.[81] Moreover, marijuana offenses increased in Colorado elementary schools 34 percent from 2012 to 2014.[82]

But what about the impact on other crimes? The expectation that legalized and commercially available marijuana would result in less crime just has not materialized—in fact, the opposite happened. Even in Holland, often promoted as an enlightened culture that allows the use of marijuana in "coffee shops," the government has made efforts to make the coffee shops smaller and easier to control in order to "combat the nuisance and crime associated with coffee shops and the trade in drugs."[83] In America, no city epitomizes Colorado's legalization effort more than its largest city—Denver. The following statistics reflect the increase in crime between 2014 and 2016 (note that 2016 was extrapolated, as the academic study only had data from January to September 2016):

robbery, 12 percent
aggravated assault, 23 percent
drugs/narcotics, 23 percent
theft from a motor vehicle (car burglaries), 31 percent

motor vehicle theft, 36 percent
murder, 55 percent
weapons violations, 57 percent
stolen property, 121 percent[84]

In fact, overall crime rates in Colorado as a whole increased 11 percent from 2013 to 2016.[85] Pop culture often portrays marijuana as some relaxing compound that at worst is part of the lifestyle of a surfer or snowboarder, often differentiating between weed and "hard drugs"—whatever that means. Although those in law enforcement are apparently not hip enough to get it, marijuana is as much a part of woke culture as climate change and plastic straws.

But there is a sinister and devastating reality to the distribution of marijuana in society, one that those promoting legalization promised would be reduced by legalizing the dealing of this psychoactive compound—the violence associated with drug dealing. Anyone can look at a statistic and see each and every murder represented simply as a number. However, police and prosecutors who investigate the murders must delve into the motivations behind the murders—who was involved and the facts surrounding their commission. The RMHIDTA report contained the following observation from Colorado Springs district attorney Dan May:

> "Colorado Springs Police Department . . . had 22 homicides in Colorado Springs last year, 2016. Eight of those were directly marijuana." During the public announcement [of the indictment of several people for large-scale marijuana distribution] May explained that authorities are overwhelmed having to deal with the crime that is associated with marijuana and claimed that "marijuana is the gateway drug to homicide."[86]

Police officers and prosecutors are without the luxury of a theoretical discussion in a student union, and their experience is not limited to a policy statement from the stage during a lecture. One simply needs to respond to, investigate, and prosecute crime to actually understand it. Sowell once wrote that intellectuals dismiss firsthand knowledge as "prejudices" or "stereotypes" in favor of the abstract beliefs of the intelligentsia.[87] The law enforcement community knows full well what the widespread availability of marijuana does to the community it is charged to protect. In 2016, Colorado Springs police conducted eight death notifications, and Dan May met with the families of eight homicide victims—victims whose lives were ended directly because of marijuana. Ask any cop or prosecutor—those meetings are anything but "abstract."

Black Market

Conventional decriminalization wisdom would say that by legalizing the drug, the black market, and the related crime associated with the illegality of the drug, would virtually disappear. However, the Colorado highway interdiction of illegal marijuana increased 43 percent for the four-year average of 2013–16 when compared to the four years prior to legalization.[88] Beyond that, Colorado drug task forces seized 1,489 pounds of illegal marijuana in 2013, but by 2016, those same task forces had seized 7,115 pounds.[89] The task forces seized 7,290 marijuana plants in 2013, but by 2016, the task forces had seized 47,108 illegal marijuana plants, and the task forces made 138 felony arrests in marijuana investigations in 2013 but nearly doubled the arrests to 252 by 2016.[90] The increase in seizure of illegal marijuana concentrate (hash oil) increased 1,099 percent from 2015 to 2016 alone.[91] And the U.S. Postal Service averaged 52 parcels of illegally shipped marijuana in the four-year average prior to Colorado's legalization, but the four years following legalization saw parcel interception rise to 491 parcels interdicted annually.[92]

Oregon's commercialized recreational marijuana

industry produces five to ten times the marijuana that could be consumed by its recreational users.[93] That surplus amounts to a black market value of $7.9 billion.[94] It should not be surprising that in the first two and a half years after recreational commercial laws went into effect, police interdicted several metric tons of Oregon black market marijuana destined for thirty-seven separate states while also seizing tens of millions of dollars in related currency.[95] One can only wonder how much of this marijuana produced under the personal, recreational use paradigm evaded detection as it made its way into the hands of our nation's children and mentally ill.

Colorado's data are a wrecking ball to any notion that legalizing a drug results in elimination of the black market—in fact, no factor in our nation's history is a bigger boon to the black market of a drug than the creation of a legal paradigm as a cover for illegal production and distribution.

Other Impacts on the Community

The negative consequences of legalized marijuana are not limited merely to increases in crime, poison control calls, hospitalizations, and consumption by children. This chapter has covered a number of negative impacts associated with marijuana legalization, but the following information deserves at least a passing mention when discussing the impact of legalized marijuana.

- With respect to the argument that marijuana use would displace the use of other legal intoxicants, after legalization in Colorado in 2012, per capita alcohol consumption increased.[96]
- Large businesses in Colorado had to seek out-of-state residents after legalization because of an insufficient number of workers who could pass a drug test.[97] Not surprisingly, accidents, injuries, absenteeism, and disciplinary problems are

significantly higher for workers who use marijuana,[98] and the percentage of workers who miss work "because they just didn't want to be there" for the overall population is 7.4 percent, but for marijuana users, the percentage is more than twice that, at 15 percent.[99]

- With the overall U.S. homeless population decreasing between 2013 and 2014, Colorado experienced an increase in homelessness.[100] In Denver, shelter usage grew 50 percent, and shelter personnel estimated that 20–30 percent of the newcomers were in Denver for easy access to marijuana.[101]

- A word to the wise: any time—*any time*—something is promoted with the promise of public revenue (typically, education funding is the most popular promise), one should immediately be suspect of the entire effort. To that end, the legalization of marijuana was promoted with the promise to line the public coffers with significant revenue. Following are the percentages of respective state budgets marijuana revenues accounted for:

  Colorado, 0.78 percent
  Washington, 0.30 percent
  Oregon, 0.24 percent
  Alaska, 0.12 percent
  California, 0.20 percent[102]

And if alcohol and tobacco are going to act as a model, the criminal justice and public health costs of alcohol and tobacco are more than ten times greater than the tax revenue collected.[103]

Conclusion

Science, and common sense, for that matter, tells us that if X leads to Y, more X equates to more Y; scientific studies have been done on marijuana's impact on mental health and drug use, albeit on weed much, much less potent than our current marijuana. Beyond that, we have several years of data on the impact the legalization of marijuana has on a state at virtually every level. So, one must ask whether the current explosion in mental health issues, homelessness, and drug addiction (and the downstream effects thereof) is only the tip of the iceberg. If so, our nation must change its course or, much like those who discounted the vulnerability of the *Titanic,* we, too, will fast move toward a historic disaster.

7

A Lesson in History
Where Did the Meth Labs Go?

The One-Pot Epidemic

Beginning around 2009, northeastern Oklahoma, predominantly the Tulsa, Oklahoma, metro area, began to experience a massive increase in clandestine methamphetamine labs. The cleanup efforts were taxing the resources of law enforcement so much that the Oklahoma Bureau of Narcotics needed to place a series of hazardous materials containers throughout the region. The agency also had to certify its agents to handle the hazardous chemicals and safely store them until professional chemical disposal contractors could arrive to take possession of the waste produced during the manufacturing process. This particular manufacturing method utilized a single reaction vessel and was commonly known as a "one-pot" or "shake and bake."

The manufacturing process can be explained quite simply. Pseudoephedrine is the active ingredient in many over-the-counter decongestants, but the pseudoephedrine molecule closely resembles methamphetamine in its base form. If fact, if one simply removes an oxygen and hydrogen group from a pseudoephedrine molecule, the resulting substance is base methamphetamine. If that sounds simple, it's because it is—that's why an idiot with three teeth and a mullet can make meth so easily. The one-pot manufacturer accom-

plishes this reaction by placing the cold medicine (pseudoephedrine) in a solvent and adding a reactive metal (typically
lithium metal strips from batteries) and ammonia (created
from ammonium nitrate in cold packs). This combination
causes a chemical reaction that does not require the application of any external heat, an exothermic reaction, oftentimes referred to as a "cold cook." It would be a misnomer
to call the preceding process a recipe, as it is a reduction
reaction—simply reducing the pseudoephedrine molecule to
methamphetamine. From 2006 to 2010, pseudoephedrine
sales at Tulsa-area Walmarts increased tenfold—a staggering 1,000 percent. As such, it would stand to reason that
90 percent of the pseudoephedrine sales were the result of
efforts to clandestinely manufacture methamphetamine.

It is crucial to acknowledge that the externalities of meth
labs are not limited to generating vast amounts of hazardous waste, which, if not intercepted by law enforcement
and legally disposed of at great cost, was destined to be
improperly discarded, thereby polluting the environment.
But the manufacturing event requires a reactive metal that
is so volatile that its simple interaction with water vapor can
cause it to spark—which can be catastrophic if such sparks
occur near large amounts of flammable vapors from the
organic solvents used in the manufacturing process, such
as ether from starting fluid or petroleum oil from camp
fuel. In fact, many of the meth labs intercepted by author-
ities were discovered by first responders to reported fires.
Owing to the frequency of fires, several of the Tulsa Fire
Department (TFD) fire marshals needed to be certified to
process meth labs. TFD worked so many meth lab fires that
some of its fire marshals became instructors at narcotic
conferences. The frequency of the meth lab fires prompted
the Oklahoma legislature to amend the first degree felony
murder statute to include deaths resulting from the meth
manufacturing process.

One manufacturer, out on bond for a previous effort
to manufacture meth, attempted to conduct the entire

manufacturing process inside of a Walmart. The responding Tulsa police officer was chemically burned when
responding to the suspicious activity reported by store
employees—indeed, injuries to officers responding to meth
labs are not uncommon.[1] Unfortunately, the societal chaos
from this manufacturing epidemic was not limited simply
to the self-destruction of the tweakers, the drain on law
enforcement resources, injury to officers, and damage
to the environment; the impact on the children of the
manufacturers was devastating. It was commonplace for
police officers to take children present at meth labs into
protective custody, as children were present at more than
one-third of the labs in Tulsa. Dr. Penny Grant, an assistant professor at the University of Oklahoma, conducted
a study and found that children removed from meth labs
tested positive for methamphetamine 71 percent of the
time with a urine sample drawn an average of 2.45 hours
after removal from the lab.[2]

Beyond the chemical exposures, the pervasive lab fires
were a danger that soon became anything but a theoretical
concern. At the beginning of the epidemic, TFD captain
Michael Baker made the following statement after a meth
lab burst into flames in a house holding five adults and two
children: "We've had two fatalities already, and we've got two
hanging onto their lives. . . . It's become a regular event."[3]

And most tragic of all, labs increased, fires persisted,
and the Tulsa County District Attorney's Office soon found
itself prosecuting multiple murders for children killed in
fires resulting from meth labs.[4]

Even the most staunch libertarian would not promote the
legalization of clandestinely manufacturing methamphetamine; clandestine methamphetamine production passes
about every test Hayek and Friedman have for the necessity
of outlawing conduct, as outlined in chapter 4. The protection of children and the impact on the environment are obvious, not to mention the resultant crime from the rampant
drug use also documented in chapter 4. Furthermore, the

costs to the public of incarcerating manufacturers, not just for the manufacturing event, but for the criminal charges of child neglect and even murder are staggering; according to the corrections department, a single ten-year sentence costs taxpayers more than $250,000. (Again, in chapter 4, cost estimates by both the right and the left are shown to be extremely misleading.) The drain on public resources resulting from the manufacturing epidemic is profound when adding up nothing more than hazardous waste cleanup costs and child welfare expenditures for the custody, fostering, and health care of manufacturers' children who became wards of the state.

But in present-day Tulsa, meth labs are virtually nonexistent. After responding to 315 labs in 2009 and 431 in 2011, the Tulsa Police Department responded to only 2 labs in 2019.[5] At present, no children are dying in fires from meth labs; no children are being routed to foster care at ballooning public expense; and the prisons are absent the scores of manufacturers taking up prison beds, as no individuals are currently being arrested for clandestinely producing methamphetamine. The savings to public expenditures from the cessation of manufacturing activity is certainly in the hundreds of millions of dollars. Clearly something caused this dramatic turnaround—not simply a tamping down of the crisis but a virtual elimination of the problem altogether. Whatever the reason for the success, everyone should seek to learn from it, replicate it, and implement similar efforts toward other drug crises. Did Oklahoma legalize manufacturing, which would validate a libertarian view of drug policy? Did Oklahoma invest millions in drug treatment? *Where did the meth labs go?*

Operation Cast Net

As we have outlined, the manufacturing process requires pseudoephedrine. In fact, a single blister pack of twenty-count

120 milligram pseudoephedrine tablets contains a total of 2.4 grams of pseudoephedrine. In the reduction reaction outlined in the preceding section, a manufacturer can pull about 90 percent of the pseudoephedrine into base methamphetamine—therefore, a box with 2.4 grams of pseudoephedrine can result in more than 2 grams of pure methamphetamine. While there may be an infinite number of methods to remove the OH (oxygen–hydrogen) group from the pseudoephedrine molecule to make base methamphetamine, every method requires pseudoephedrine.

Beginning in 2004, pseudoephedrine was sold behind the counter only at pharmacies, with limitations placed on the daily and monthly amounts that could be purchased. This became national policy as a result of the first wave of "Uncle Fester" meth labs that ravaged the nation and are discussed later in this chapter. With the development of the one-pot manufacturing method, a single box could be used to manufacture a much smaller yield. But as pseudoephedrine sales were limited to a few grams per month, a demand grew for pseudoephedrine purchased from pharmacies. By 2011, a single box of pseudoephedrine had a street value of a half gram of meth, or $50. For some reason, the one-pot epidemic in Oklahoma was confined to the Tulsa area. While the busiest pharmacy in Oklahoma City sold no more than five boxes a day, pharmacies in Tulsa averaged seventy.

The individuals purchasing pseudoephedrine for one-pot labs were called "smurfs." *Smurf* was a money laundering term used to describe a group of people who spread out to deposit illicit money at multiple locations to avoid suspicion. In the same fashion, groups of people sourcing pseudoephedrine would go on trips to purchase the cold medication at multiple locations. The groups would exit a car at a pharmacy, make efforts to appear not to be associated with one another, purchase the pseudoephedrine in the stores, then return to the car separately—a smurfing method law enforcement officers would dub the "clown car."

From November 4 to 8, 2011, approximately 200 officers coordinated an effort to intercept manufacturers sourcing pseudoephedrine at twenty pharmacies in northeast Oklahoma, including fourteen locations in Tulsa County. So, with no specific information whatsoever, what did officers find at these twenty locations? During this four-day effort named Operation Cast Net, officers arrested 334 people attempting to source pseudoephedrine for the production of methamphetamine. The operation included pursuits, firearm seizures, arrests of homeless people enticed by the allure of easy money, and even a pregnant female who admitted to regularly ingesting methamphetamine (as was her fetus, no doubt).

The sheer number of people involved in manufacturing at just twenty pharmacies over the course of a few days is shocking in and of itself, especially considering the havoc meth labs were wreaking on the Tulsa area. Yet the most shocking aspect of Operation Cast Net is what happened immediately following the arrests.

The Email

Officers in northeastern Oklahoma as well as their resources were getting overrun by the meth lab explosion and the downstream consequences. Oregon had faced a very similar problem, but once pseudoephedrine was made prescription only, Oregon's lab problem disappeared. There was a similar movement in the Oklahoma legislature to make pseudoephedrine a prescription-only medication. However, a group of businesses were profiting immensely from the 1,000 percent increase in sales, so lobbyists from the pharmaceutical industry sought to stop the effort by cozying up to legislators, and a public propaganda campaign was instituted, including commercials with a female voice claiming the government wanted her to go to the doctor simply to get over-the-counter cold medication for her children. Amazingly, the advocacy of children was used as a talking point for nixing the same solution that had already protected so many children in Oregon. So, *Operation Cast Net* was designed by the Oklahoma Bureau of Narcotics along with the bureau's numerous partners in policing and prosecution to demonstrate the negative impact of pseudoephedrine availability. In a few days at only twenty pharmacies, law enforcement had prevented more than 300 of these horrendous manufacturing events. Sadly, legislative leadership at the Oklahoma capitol completely kept the bill from being heard. Discouraged, the peace officers and prosecutors went about their jobs, almost resolving themselves to one-pot labs remaining a part of their world for the extended future. But the public information officer of the Oklahoma Bureau of Narcotics, officed hours away in Oklahoma City headquarters, sent an email to all Bureau agents almost exactly a year later:

> After a 3 year increase due to "One Pot" labs, especially in northeastern Oklahoma we've seen a remarkable drop in meth labs seizures for 12 consecutive months. As you can see from the stats below, meth labs in Tulsa County (the meth lab hot spot for the past 3 years) have dropped from 371 November through October of last year to 250 from November through October of this year. This trend began 8 months before the new PSE [pseudoephedrine] limits took effect this summer, plus NPLEX [a pseudoephedrine tracking database] hasn't started yet, so obviously there are other factors for the drop. Hopefully, this trend will continue.

Initially, I only glanced at the email, paying little attention. I had been so discouraged by the failure of our legislature to act that I had mentally checked out on meth labs. But then I saw a copy of the email forwarded to me by an extremely talented Bureau agent and good friend, Mitch Smith, who attributed the decline to Operation Cast Net. As

I thought about my current work as a drug agent, I realized that the number of meth labs had in fact greatly subsided in recent months. Then I began to look at the data and noticed immediately—*immediately*—that after Operation Cast Net was the precise time when the pseudoephedrine sales dropped dramatically. One of the most active sites for pseudoephedrine sales was Muskogee, Oklahoma. Muskogee, about forty-five minutes from Tulsa and famous for the Merle Haggard song "We Don't Smoke Marijuana in Muskogee," has a tremendous narcotics unit stacked with a slew of good operators and a fantastic supervisor. But in 2011, tweakers in Muskogee, like in the rest of northeast Oklahoma, were smoking (and injecting) meth. Muskogee was one of the Cast Net sites, and that operation was run by the Muskogee Police Department's Special Investigation Unit. Figure 1 charts pseudoephedrine sales for the Muskogee Walmart, with a dramatic drop in sales evident immediately following Operation Cast Net.

In narcotics work, the numbers and statistics tell a story, but one that is wholly incomplete. Drug activity is by its nature cloaked in secrecy, and its participants do not just avoid reporting their activity but go to great lengths to conceal it. So, in drug work, intelligence from narcotics operators is the single greatest asset. Narcs do not rely on numbers; they rely on information (either from drug suspects or other police officers).

I spoke to one of the most accomplished narcotics investigators in the Tulsa area, who was assigned to Tulsa's special investigations division. This officer said that ever since the widely publicized smurfing operation (Operation Cast Net) and smaller follow-up special-emphasis operations at pharmacies, meth users had stopped sourcing pseudoephedrine from pharmacies and attempting to manufacture meth. In fact, virtually all of the Cast Net team leaders attributed the cessation of smurfing and lab operations to Cast Net. To be sure, a form of methamphetamine from south of the border called "ice" was supplying the meth users both before and

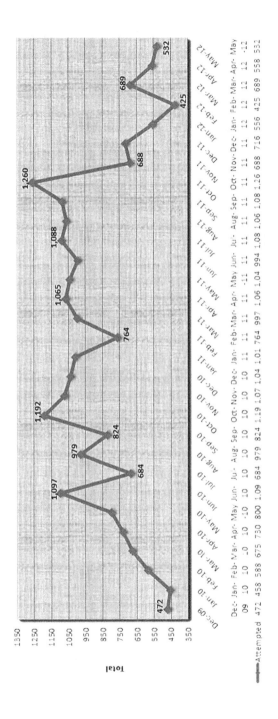

FIGURE 1. Muskogee Walmart pseudoephedrine sales.

after the one-pot epidemic, but narcotics officers can attack the commercially based black market more easily than thousands of individual cells where the creation and end use of the drug entailed only a handful of people. This much was clear, both in the numbers and in reports by narcotics professionals: a dedicated and targeted enforcement effort made sourcing lab-bound pseudoephedrine more difficult for smurfs, such that lab operations ultimately ceased altogether—and northeastern Oklahoma was monumentally better off because of the deliberate efforts of several dozen police officers and prosecutors.

Other Historical Methamphetamine Manufacturing Trends

The one-pot epidemic is only one of several methamphetamine lab trends. In the 1980s, the predominant domestic manufacturing process was by phenyl-2-propanone (P2P). The P2P method required a number of chemicals, which meth cooks would get from industrial chemical supply stores. After Drug Enforcement Administration (DEA) efforts at undercover storefronts and federal legislation relating to the regulation of required chemicals, P2P labs disappeared overnight.

In the 1990s, the first wave of the ephedrine/pseudoephedrine reduction process hit the United States, especially the Midwest. Pseudoephedrine was a simple over-the-counter medication. Again, by removing that simple oxygen–hydrogen group from the molecule, the manufacturer could create methamphetamine in its base form. From the late 1990s to the mid-2000s, the primary processes by which meth manufacturers accomplished this chemical reaction were through heating the cold medication with red phosphorus and iodine or using a reactive metal with anhydrous ammonia (typically stolen from farmers' fertilizer tanks) without the necessity of heat. At the beginning of the meth lab epidemic, labs were overseen by the "cook," that individual who had the knowledge to accomplish the reaction. But after a few years, the concept of the cook began to erode—everyone knew how to manufacture methamphetamine. This was due in large part to dissemination of the "recipe" on the internet and an underground book by an author calling himself "Uncle Fester."

As the manufacturing events grew, the sale of pseudoephedrine at truck stops, discount stores, and especially convenience stores grew tremendously—such that wholesalers dealing exclusively in cheap pseudoephedrine tablets working from their garages became millionaires. At the time, meth labs were tearing the Midwest apart—child neglect, crimes to support addiction, and strained public safety resources contributed to a crisis unlike any the nation had previously experienced.

But as we have learned, the manufacturing process requires pseudoephedrine—though the chemical reaction could be conducted in a thousand ways, each requires pseudoephedrine. Public safety professionals, police, and prosecutors who witnessed firsthand the devastation of meth labs knew how to halt the crisis. In 2004, Oklahoma passed a law, known as House Bill 2176, that made pseudoephedrine sellable only at pharmacies and placed it behind the counter. Furthermore, the law limited how much a person could purchase at any one time as well as within any thirty-day period. Those limits were in excess of the maximum recommended daily intake but far less than manufactures would need to produce methamphetamine. Immediately after implementation of the law, meth labs in Oklahoma dropped 70 percent. Other states that were similarly devastated by meth labs passed similar laws, and once surrounding states enacted like legislation, meth labs dropped over 90 percent.

The preceding examples prompt a clear takeaway—this nation has faced a crisis relating to the manufacture of methamphetamine on three separate occasions. In each instance, the problem was solved, and by solved, I mean the problem was over 99 percent eliminated. It was not some newfangled social science proposal or adherence to an economic theory that solved the crises but the first-hand knowledge of men and women of public safety, in each and every case. Certain laws were passed, those laws were enforced, and the labs went away. Theorists on the right and left do not worry over or opine about meth labs today because America just doesn't have them anymore. Anyone who objects to the passage and enforcement of drug laws should ask if our nation was better off during each of the meth lab epidemics outlined in this chapter. In the oft-maligned War on Drugs analogy, each of these meth lab crises would be a battle—a battle in which both drug laws and those enforcing them were victorious.

The Synthetic Cannabinoid Epidemic
(Spice, Incense, and K2)

A very accomplished scientist at Clemson University developed a synthetic cannabinoid during his research in the hope of determining potential benefits of the synthetic compound. This scientist, John W. Huffman, would learn from law enforcement that his namesake compound, known as JWH-018, was being detected on organic matter sold in stores as incense, which was being smoked as an alternative to marijuana. The practice began in Europe around 2006 but soon crossed the Atlantic and reached epidemic levels in the United States in just a few years.[6]

During this time, there were repeated stories of high school children having severe dystonic reactions resulting from the ingestion of the synthetic cannabinoids. Hospital emergency rooms were regularly admitting patients with seizures and bizarre reactions. Drug recognition experts examining persons under the influence of synthetic marijuana had difficulty, as the users displayed signs of having

used several different categories of drugs, including cannabis, stimulants, and/or hallucinogens.

The synthetic marijuana was sold almost exclusively at
convenience stores as incense for around $20 a gram. Yet
this incense was packaged like candy and clearly marketed
to a younger audience. Stores often made exponentially
more money from the sale of synthetic marijuana than
they did from the sale of traditional retail goods. While
the stores would deposit tens if not hundreds of thousands of dollars into their business accounts, they did not
deposit enough of the proceeds to avoid suspicion. Search
warrants for the homes of these storeowners would typically produce boxes of cash totaling additional six-figure
seizures.

But, as of the writing of this book in early 2021,
synthetic marijuana is nonexistent at convenience stores.
No helicopters are landing at schools to medivac children
who have ingested the "incense"; no hospitals are admitting users; and the destitute addict is not using these
substances, causing severe adverse reactions. Synthetic
marijuana was not legalized, the government did not invest
billions in treatment, and the absence is not attributable to
a prevention campaign. At the federal level, the substances
were outlawed via an administrative emergency sched-
uling by the administrator of the DEA. This legislative
update, coupled with a dedicated law enforcement effort
directed at the nefarious convenience stores, involving
search warrants and criminal charges, completely eradicated the problem.

Again, this nation encountered a severe drug problem
ravaging children and vulnerable populations, and the
epidemic was eradicated. The two factors that unques-
tionably led to this panacea were the illegality of the
compound and the targeted enforcement from the men
and women of law enforcement along with their prose-
cutorial partners.

Other Successes

Lucky Luciano was a mafia boss in 1930s America who dabbled in many forms of illegal activity, not the least of which was heroin trafficking. Luciano was ultimately sentenced to a decades-long prison sentence for prostitution and extortion in 1936. After assisting the U.S. military with Allied efforts in Italy around 1942, his sentence was commuted, and he was deported to his home country of Italy. Not changing his spots, Luciano used his American drug connections and went from distributing heroin in the United States to setting up a massive European heroin importation conglomerate known as the infamous French Connection. For the next several decades, the French Connection grew to distribute an estimated 95 percent of the world's heroin.[7] However, after a focused effort by American drug enforcement, including partnerships with French counterparts, more than one thousand pounds of heroin were intercepted, several clandestine heroin labs in France were dismantled, and the drug enforcement endeavor culminated with the arrest of more than three thousand members of the French drug trafficking organization in 1972 (only fifty-seven had been arrested the year before).[8] One might ask, just how did this law enforcement effort impact America? In 1973, on the East Coast of the United States, the price of heroin doubled. In fact, the heroin that was available in 1973 was only 2 to 3 percent pure, which made detoxification much easier. And what was the impact of reducing both the amount and purity of heroin? Heroin deaths dropped, the percentage of people in 1973 arrested with heroin in their systems went down, admissions to methadone clinics decreased, and most importantly, crime rates dropped dramatically.[9]

This much is certain: both the existence of drug policy and the enforcement thereof dramatically impact the rates of drug use, and consequently drug-related crime. At cocaine's highpoint in the 1980s, 6 million Americans used the drug when measured by the past-month use metric. However, after a policy aimed at both reduction in use and targeted enforcement locally and abroad, that number has dropped to 1.5 million today.[10]

In 1960, the murder rate in America was on a decades-long decline, less than half of what it was approximately thirty years before. But the murder rate then began to rise, nearly doubling in fourteen years.[11] What happened? In the early 1960s, the normalization of heroin was widespread in the United States, exemplified both by pop culture and a resistance to enforcing drug laws. Not surprisingly, in Atlanta, the number of heroin users increased tenfold by the end of the decade. Similar numbers could be seen in Boston and Washington, D.C.[12] More importantly, drug use rates and associated violent crime nationwide steadily declined after increased penalties for drug and violent crime were instituted in the 1990s.

Perhaps no policy initiative better reflects the positive impact of enforcement in the latter part of the twentieth century than the experience of New York City. In the 1980s, New York City was plagued by murders, robberies, drug crimes, and theft. But the city experienced a turnaround unlike any seen in our nation's history. Newly elected mayor Rudolph Guliani and his police commissioner, William Joseph Bratton, oversaw an important effort based on a policing theory dubbed Broken Windows. The "Broken Windows" essay was penned in 1982 by sociologists James Q. Wilson and George L. Kelling. The theory urged that disorder and crime are linked, that untended nuisance behavior leads to a breakdown in community controls, and that serious crime follows. In essence, street crimes, including violent crimes, flourish where disorder goes unchecked. The "Broken Windows" essay essentially argued that failure to address conduct that may not have a direct victim will lead to significantly greater disorder, violence, and victimization.

So what happened with the new effort? University of California law professor Franklin Zimring called the reduction in New York City's crime rate "one of the most remarkable stories in the history of urban crime."[13] In 1993, the year before Giuliani took office, there were 26.5 murders and 2,083.3 violent crimes per 100,000 people. By 2001, the murder rate had dropped to 8.9 per 100,000 (a reduction of 66.4 percent), and violent crime had dropped to 927.5 per 100,000 (a reduction of 55.6 percent).[14]

While national crime rates were also reduced during this period (commensurate with stiffer penalties for a host of offenses, including drug charges), New York City's progress greatly outpaced the national averages. Most important here is that Giuliani and Bratton instituted a campaign to reduce crime through basic enforcement, which led to reductions in violent crime greater than initiatives focused solely on more serious offenses.

Failures

It stands to reason that if enforcement of law has a positive impact, then the lack of enforcement will result in negative consequences. Perhaps we should stick with New York. "Bail reform" is the most recent fad promoted among criminal justice reform advocates, and New York was the first state to institute this "reform," which mandated the release of misdemeanor offenders and other "nonviolent" suspects. Both police and prosecutors, those who deal with these offenders every day, warned that this effort would have disastrous consequences—regardless of the euphemisms used to describe these offenders, the cases involved victims, and removing the consequence of detention for the crime would embolden these deviants. But the practice was lauded by the media with statements much like the following:

> On April 1, 2019, New York State passed sweeping criminal justice reform legislation that eliminates money bail and pretrial detention for nearly all misdemeanor and

nonviolent felony cases. The measure goes into effect in January 2020.[15]

Another criminal justice reform group stated the following after the passage of the bail reform: "a preliminary analysis suggests that the bail reform law will significantly reduce pretrial detention."[16] But almost immediately after implementation, the crime rate in New York City skyrocketed. By early February 2020, a few weeks after implementation, even liberal mayor Bill de Blasio, a proponent of the "reform," admitted that the bail reform act was responsible for the increase in crime.[17]

Another recent example can be found in my home state of Oklahoma, typically regarded as a very "red" state. In that regard, after a coordinated messaging campaign, voters passed a left-leaning state question that reduced every drug possession to a misdemeanor and increased the threshold amount for a property crime to constitute a felony. In Oklahoma, any advocacy group can propose any legislative amendment to the law after obtaining the requisite number of signatures; the public does not vote on the actual text of the law, as only a short summary of the legislative changes appears on the ballot. State Question 780, dubbed by its proponents as Oklahoma Smart Justice Reform, was a mere paragraph drafted by those who sought its passage.

The state question, which went into effect in July 2017, also removed the enhancing ability, which in effect treated an offender with dozens of theft convictions the same as a first-time offender. In essence, State Question 780 took every single possession of narcotics and theft under $1,000 offense and transformed those crimes into a traffic ticket, punishable no more than driving without a valid driver's license. The companion ballot issue, State Question 781, was a proposal to redirect all of the money saved from these offensive incarcerations to local governments to fund rehabilitation of the purported scores of drug possessors filling up Oklahoma's prisons. State Question 781 was summarized in the bold aspiration that for the first time in our republic's history, a government bureaucracy would tell its legislative body that the agency received too much money and would send it back. Not surprisingly, three years later, no such "saved" monies have been sent to local governments.

It did not take long for the results to become evident. The Oklahoma Retail Crime Association conducted a survey of 11 Oklahoma retailers constituting 272 physical locations. The results were depressingly mind-boggling:

> Between 2016 and 2018, the surveyed retailers reported that known theft incidents increased 64 percent, the number of shoplifters reported to law enforcement increased by an average of 47 percent, known losses to theft increased 37 percent, and the average amount stolen per shoplifting incident increased 57 percent.[18]

QuikTrip is a very successful convenience store franchise with locations throughout the United States and is head-quartered in Tulsa. A spokesperson for QuikTrip was interviewed by the media several months after passage of the so-called reform:

> "Being from Tulsa, Oklahoma, having our headquarters here, we're kind of embarrassed by how bad crime is getting right now," said Mike Thornbrugh, spokesperson for QT. Thornbrugh said thefts skyrocketed not long after Oklahoma voters approved "State Question 780." There are QT's all over the country and Thornbrugh said, "We'll tell you Tulsa, Oklahoma is the worst in regards to property crime in any city or state that we operate."[19]

Thornbrugh later testified at a legislative interim study and said the following:

> The property crimes last year have increased over 300%

... and the lost inventory in Oklahoma is four times higher than anywhere else that we operate.[20]

Proponents of this social justice reform measure were quick to disown any impact from their decriminalization of property and drug crime. This assault on reality had two components. First, the association of decriminalization with increased crime was challenged in that shoplifting at retail outlets was overwhelming for misdemeanor amounts before State Question 780, and the typical shoplifting case would have been a misdemeanor both before and after State Question 780. The problem with this position is twofold. First, it assumes that property crime has no connection to drug use. Second, in reality, State Question 780 removed police and prosecutor's ability to deal with repeat offenders. Theft and drug possessions were reduced to the punishment for driving without a valid driver's license. As a result, drug use increased, the property crime associated with drug use increased, law enforcement had no ability to intervene, and the same criminals committed the crimes again and again. The unassailable fact that drug crimes are supported by property crimes is outlined in this book, and the notion that drug use and property crime each exists in an independent vacuum ignores decades of real experience.

The second challenge to the clear negative impact of decriminalization after State Question 780 took effect was the statement that such thefts were not consistent with the officially reported crime statistics, which showed an 11 percent increase in theft. Again, it is quite a random event to catch a thief, so reported thefts are not at all reflective of the frequency of thefts. Clearly the most accurate measure of theft (contrasting those actually caught with the more realistic number of those who evade detection) is inventory loss. It is truly amazing that social justice advocates would tell retailers that they were not experiencing the theft they were experiencing. Dan Smalgio, president of the Oklahoma

Retail Crime Association, explained the gap between actual theft and law enforcement reporting:

> [The reason theft reporting numbers are not higher is because retailers] only report a fraction of the cases to law enforcement.
>
> There are several factors that lead retailers to not report thefts. In particular, the reporting process for a single theft can take two hours, which translates into retailer costs that can exceed the value of the item stolen.
>
> Most of our retailers don't even report a case of $50 or $100. . . . It's not a valuable use of our time. I'm not going to spend $70 worth of payroll to report a $50 theft.[21]

Dubious recitations of statistics are often used to validate a social justice warrior's narrative. One would think that merchants would be the most informed on increases and decreases of theft at their stores, but the social justice advocates simply denied any increase in shoplifting. Those lauding the decriminalization of theft and drug possession never offered a motive for these merchants to fabricate their experiences. Regarding the overall feeling of Oklahoma merchants, Smalgio stated,

> We were unable to find a single retailer, whether they participated in the survey or not, that reported that theft was flat or down during that period. . . . Every one of them expressed concern that theft was not only up, but way up.[22]

This gap between actual theft and reported theft is easy to understand, especially for public safety professionals and merchants drawing from their experience. In January 2020, I interviewed a heroin user who was contemplating becoming an informant. As this very issue was percolating in policy centers, I asked him about his heroin habit. He said that he used about $100 per day for three years, yet he had no job or income during that time. When I asked him how he funded his habit, he said he stole items from retail outlets around the Tulsa area and returned the stolen merchandise for a refund, then used that money to buy heroin. He minimized and said he only did that about three times per week. While his math falls far short to support his habit, let's assume it to be correct. This addict's description of funding his drug use amounts to more than 150 theft events totaling more than $45,000. And during all of his shoplifting efforts, this individual said he was detected only one time by store personnel—and this detection did not result in his arrest. The preceding story illustrates the reality of drug-inspired theft—it is very pervasive, and it is difficult to get caught. Social policy advocates have every incentive to deny evidence counter to their view of the world or the wisdom of their edicts. But a merchant has no motive to fabricate inventory loss resulting from theft, just a motive to preserve the livelihood of his or her industry.

George Orwell once said that "some ideas are so stupid, only an intellectual could believe them." One would be hard-pressed to find a better representation of Orwell's edict than the argument that decriminalizing crime will result in criminals committing less crime.

The evidence could not be more definitive regarding the association with law enforcement and order. Even studies from groups on the left found that misdemeanor enforcement led to a reduction in felony arrests and incarcerations in New York.[23] During the 1960s, there was a push to reduce prison sentences and deemphasize crimes intellectuals deemed nonviolent. In fact, the prison population went from 212,000 to 196,000. But the rate of violent crime per one hundred thousand people more than doubled from 1960 to 1970.[24] In Washington, D.C., during that decade, serious crime increased 400 percent, and it should be noted that heroin use increased 1,000 percent in our nation's capital. Murders in Detroit went up fivefold during the 1960s.[25]

California had a similar experience when, following efforts to release large numbers of inmates, California's spikes in crime outpaced the rest of the United States.[26] When Jean-Jacques Rousseau wrote *The Social Contract,* he said, "Frequent pardons signalize that crimes will soon need no pardon; and anyone can see what that must lead to."[27] Curiously, what was so obvious and clear to Rousseau (to "anyone," as he put it) more than 250 years ago is not even acknowledged as a possibility by twentieth-century social justice advocates.

President Obama's chief of staff Rahm Emanuel became mayor of Chicago in 2011 and, with the fervor of an enlightened intellectual, ceased stop-and-frisk practices that had been used to make poor neighborhoods safer. In fact, Emanuel did so in the name of compassion. Yet within six months, the murder rate increased 38 percent.[28] As of the writing of this book in 2021, Chicago's violent crime rate continues to soar. New York experienced similar increases in crime when government leaders directed the cessation of stop and frisk.[29]

Clearly this nation saw a shift in emphasis on enforcing drug crimes and "nonviolent" offenses beginning around ten years ago. After a decades-long decline in both drug use and violent crime rates, the reversal of that trend should be alarming. Although violent crime is up, misdemeanor arrests are down. In 2015, a time of catastrophic surges in violent crime, low-level misdemeanor arrests (like drinking and urinating in public) were down double digits in several major cities, pushing down reduction efforts in such enforcement, up to and including locales with drug arrests, 67 percent.[30] Notably, this enforcement trend paralleled a 16 percent increase in the murder rates in sixty major American cities.[31]

Recent public campaigns lambasting police departments resulted in curtailed enforcement—and sharp increases in crime. Heather MacDonald has chronicled the devastating impacts of what has been dubbed the Ferguson Effect.

Michael Brown was portrayed by the media and advocacy groups as an innocent citizen gunned down while trying to surrender. This narrative was patently false, as Brown had just committed a robbery and was assaulting the police officer when he was shot, but that didn't stop celebrities and charlatans from repeating the debunked mantra "Hands up, don't shoot." After the propagandized outrage and attack on the police in Ferguson, nearby St. Louis saw arrests drop by one-third, while homicides increased 47 percent and robberies increased 82 percent.[32] In fact, there was a tremendous nationwide increase in violent crime in poor neighborhoods after the false narrative of biased policing began.[33]

Perhaps no greater example of the devastating societal impacts of curtailing enforcement can be seen than the recent debacle in Baltimore. Freddie Gray's arrest and subsequent death in Baltimore led to riots, as he was portrayed as an innocent minority who died as the result of police brutality. His cause of death was a severed spinal cord apparently endured in the back of a police van, but to date, exactly how he died has not been explained. While Gray may have been portrayed in the media as a member of the youth choir and an athlete, by age twenty-five, he had already been arrested on a minimum of twelve occasions, with a good deal of the arrests related to drug dealing or possession of narcotics. At the time of his arrest on April 12, 2015, he had two drug charges pending, including a distribution of heroin charge.[34]

In what could be graciously called a series of bizarre legal theories, State Attorney Marilyn Mosby charged six officers associated with Gray's arrest. Mosby said officers had "failed to establish probable cause for Mr. Gray's arrest, as no crime had been committed," and that Gray "suffered a critical neck injury as a result of being handcuffed, shackled by his feet and unrestrained inside the BPD wagon." Mosby additionally alleged that the officers were guilty of false imprisonment, because Gray was carrying a pocket knife of legal size and not the switchblade police claimed he had possessed at the time of his arrest. The officers faced an array of charges relating to Gray's death, including manslaughter and depraved heart murder. A former Baltimore prosecutor named Page Croyder wrote an op-ed published in the *Baltimore Sun* where she described Mosby's charging decision as "either incompetence or an unethical recklessness." Croyder was critical of Mosby's deviation of normal procedures and alleged that Mosby sought to "step into the national limelight" and that she "pandered to the public." After a series of acquittals, mistrials, and multiple dismissals, Mosby did not secure a single conviction, and all six officers were reinstated in good standing with the Baltimore Police Department.[35]

Baltimore was already a dangerous city plagued by drugs, crime, violence, and murder. However, after Mosby put forth a legal theory that officers could be responsible for murder if the misdemeanor arrest was found later to lack probable cause, arrests plummeted. And the impact of this reduced enforcement on these minority communities was devastating—and tragic. In 2014, Baltimore had 211 homicides. But as arrests plummeted, the murder rate rose to 344 in 2015, and Baltimore sustained five consecutive years of 300 plus homicides.[36] In Baltimore, ninety percent of the homicide victims are Black. Much has been made about Baltimore regarding the Freddie Gray ordeal. There were allegations that the manner in which public officials conducted their duties resulted in the death of a minority—in light of the evidence, someone in Baltimore has bloody hands.

A Tale of One City

I was blessed to serve on the executive board of the Association of Oklahoma Narcotic Enforcers, including several years as president or vice president. Every year, the executive boards of the state narcotic associations meet in Washington, D.C., as part of the National Narcotic Officers Association Coalition. I was honored to attend as part of the Oklahoma delegation in 2018, 2019, and 2020. In 2018, around our hotel, just blocks from Capitol Hill, we periodically observed signs of homelessness and smelled the odor of marijuana no more than two times. In 2019, the homeless population had increased, and we smelled marijuana perhaps half a dozen times during our four-day stay. By 2020, the homeless population was markedly worse. On the first morning of that year's meeting, across from our hotel on the sidewalk sat a man wrapped in blankets, wet from the rain, rolling marijuana into a "blunt" (cigar). My colleagues saw a man unconscious and in need of medical attention (an apparent overdose) and waited with him until the ambulance arrived. Walking to our hotel from dinner the first evening, I saw another homeless man in clear distress with first responders tending to him. That same night, I walked outside of a restaurant to FaceTime my children, and a mentally disturbed homeless man walked up to me and screamed something incoherent. All of those events were in the first twenty-four hours. Throughout our trip, we observed that the streets were littered with discarded clothes, trash, and foil packets from cigars (clearly from the smoking of marijuana), and we smelled marijuana so often we could not keep track.

As part of the Coalition's effort to represent its members, we spend a day on Capitol Hill meeting with our respective congressional members, reporting on public safety in our home states, and providing information to our lawmakers. My 2020 Oklahoma delegation had commented on the impressive design of the Library of Congress, the grandiose steps leading to the Supreme Court, and the beauty of the Dome—in fact, Capitol Hill is an assemblage of beautiful architecture, skilled masonry, and aesthetic beauty. The day on Capitol Hill is an exhausting one—a day full of meetings and several miles of walking across the Capitol Hill complex. As we walked back to our hotel from our hours on the Hill, I noticed we had not seen a single homeless person. I commented on this to my group of colleagues, and we collectively noticed that after days of being inundated with severe homelessness marked by drug use and mental illness, we had experienced a temporary reprieve—as if we had been in a time warp from decades before.

But then we crossed the street, leaving the Capitol grounds. And immediately—immediately—we saw several destitute homeless people, observed the trash and disgusting accessories associated with the homeless, and once again smelled the odor of marijuana. On the capitol grounds, the Capitol Police enforce federal law, and marijuana is against federal law on federal land. But Washington, D.C., had legalized marijuana, and liberal policies on enforcement foster drug use and the resultant homelessness. In the 1980s, America was familiar with the disgusting squalor of a crack house—by 2020, a combination of legalized marijuana and lax enforcement had turned Washington, D.C., into a virtual crack house.

And the irony hit me like a punch—there we were, traveling to Washington, D.C., to tell lawmakers that drug law and its enforcement will make our communities noticeably safer and better. We didn't need to cite the West Coast both before and after drug legalization or outline the debilitating statistics from Denver after the legalization of marijuana, because the single greatest example of the visible devastation caused by reducing drug laws and their enforcement was our nation's capital itself.

False Comparisons to Prohibition

Perhaps no single talking point is more popular among those seeking to legalize drugs than the comparison to Prohibition. But before engaging in this analysis, it is imperative to define exactly what is being discussed. That is, precisely what are we talking about when we say "legaliza-tion"? Unless one advocates for the freedom of a metham-phetamine addict to manufacture methamphetamine in a clandestine lab reacting in a house full of children, the need for the state to prohibit certain conduct is clear. The meth cook endangering children is at one end of the spectrum, and the ingestion of sugary drinks lies at the other. There-fore the debate over regulating substances is where society should draw the line, be it at sugar, tobacco, alcohol, mari-juana, hallucinogenic drugs, or PCP—a discussion regarding which substance-using conduct is merely self-destructive and which substance-using conduct infringes on others. That is a discussion law enforcement professionals are well equipped to have.

Second, the oft repeated opening salvo of Prohibition comparisons is that Prohibition didn't work. Again, we must define the term *work*. Prohibition had a fourteen-year reign in the United States, from 1920 to 1933. But during that time, alcohol consumption in the United States dropped between 30 and 50 percent and stayed low for decades. As Jeffrey Stamm noted,

> admission to state mental hospitals for alcoholic psycho-sis declined from 10.1 per 100,000 in 1911 to 4.7 in 1928. Arrests for public drunkenness and disorderly conduct declined 50 percent between 1916 and 1922.[37]

In fact, criminologist James Q. Wilson found that Prohi-bition "may have been the single most effective effort in American history to change human behavior by plan."[38] To be absolutely clear, this book is not advocating the rein-statement of alcohol prohibition but is simply challenging the proposition that merely claiming Prohibition didn't "work" ignores the fact that the use rates of alcohol and the negative effects of alcohol abuse were significantly reduced.

But the superficiality of the comparison to outlawing contemporary drugs to early twentieth-century prohibition is not limited to the malleability of the terms—addictive psychoactive compounds bear no resemblance to other vices. Anyone who promotes liberty of the individual abhors the nanny state, and this book makes no effort to infringe on individual liberty. As destructive as it may be, a person should be free to consume tobacco or eat sugary foods. Although such practices impact the health care costs to the nation as a whole, that is a function of failed health care policies contrary to libertarian theory. But drug use by its nature impacts third parties at alarming rates. It is precisely the individual liberty of those who do not use drugs that drug laws protect. Alcohol users simply do not break into cars, commit repeated shoplifting, or engage in armed robberies to support their consumption—not even the most addicted of alcoholics. While there may be functional alcoholics, the notion of a "functional" meth addict or a heroin junkie who holds down a job is about as well documented as the Loch Ness monster. And drugs cost money. Unlike recreational alcohol consumers, drug users fund their habit by stealing from those who do work. And while virtually no one would promote the raising of children in a home marred by alcohol abuse, even fewer would acknowledge the vastly greater adverse consequences of abuse and neglect directed toward children raised in a drug-addicted household, assuming the children were not removed and made wards of the state.

We tend to view history in terms of a U.S.-centric perspective, as if the United States is the only nation with any experience in seeking to restrict drug use. Nearly a century ago, the League of Nations passed international restrictions on the production and use of opium as well as opium's derivative, heroin.[39] While our nation realized the dangers of psychoactive drugs and passed the Harrison Narcotics Act of 1914,[40] Mexico outlawed marijuana seventeen years before the United States based in large part on associations between marijuana use and mental illness.[41] In fact, despite the cultural use of peyote and salvia, as far back as the 1800s, Mexico associated marijuana use with mental illness and violence,[42] which was also documented in 1908 when a writer for the *Boston Medical Journal* noticed mental illness in Mexican mining camps caused by marijuana use.[43] Meanwhile, Europe, long heralded as enlightened in its progressive views on drug use, has been trending toward increased penalties for drug offenses.[44] Alex Berenson points out that the positive feelings toward marijuana are an American and Canadian phenomenon, while Europe as a whole has seen marijuana use decrease with the increasing volume of evidence regarding its negative impacts—a phenomenon he calls the "transatlantic knowledge gap."[45]

To be sure, our drug use is much higher than it is among our Western counterparts, and the downstream impacts of drug use are also exponentially greater. But that would hardly be a reason to institute policy that would necessarily lead to even more drug use, which would increase every negative impact drug use has on our community.

Outlawing drugs has a purpose much deeper than any effort to punish the dealers and users. The American Society of Addictive Medicine (ASAM) has clearly stated that once a substance is legalized, its perceived danger is reduced, which leads to increased use of the substance, and that use rates increase when a drug is made more available.[46] Furthermore, as Jeffrey Stamm has noted, "the epidemic of dope is constantly held in check by both the objective risk of punishment and subjective sense of wrongdoing."[47] Put more simply, Mark Klieman made clear that the prohibition on drug use clearly prevents their massive abuse.[48]

Dr. Kevin Sabet was formerly employed by the White House's Office of National Drug Control Policy (i.e., the office of the Drug Tsar). He formed a nonprofit organization known as Smart Approaches to Marijuana (SAM) to combat the normalization of marijuana resulting from the barrage of legalization efforts. Sabet points out that while in excess of seventy-thousand Americans die each year from opiate overdoses, hundreds of thousands more die each and every year from smoking cigarettes. However, if a parent were given the choice between their adolescent smoking one cigarette and injecting a dose of heroin, clearly the parent would want the child to smoke the cigarette.[49] Dr. Sabet's point is resounding—smoking tobacco kills more Americans than opioids because of the widespread consumption of cigarettes, and despite being legal, cigarettes are far from safe; the same can be said of alcohol. Again, this book makes no effort to restrict the use of tobacco—one should be free to engage in the unhealthy habit of inhaling carcinogens or chewing tobacco even if such uses exponentially increase the chances of getting cancer. With the advent of designated smoking areas reducing secondhand smoke exposure, the negative impacts of tobacco use are overwhelmingly limited to the user—not so with drug use, and not by a very long shot.

Comparisons between alcohol and marijuana or other drugs also ignore the respective use rates. Oftentimes, advocates for marijuana will argue that alcohol use leads to more crime than marijuana consumption, but such proclamations are based on total tabulations and ignore the fact that exponentially more Americans consume alcohol in relation to cannabis. In fact, the association of marijuana use to violence is greater than it is for alcohol—a fact conveniently ignored during any prohibition comparison.[50]

Approximately 20 percent of marijuana users engage in daily use, while only one in fifteen people who use alcohol do so daily.[51] After commercializing recreational marijuana, its daily use rate in Oregon skyrocketed to a staggering 31 percent.[52] Tracking with the national movement to legalize marijuana, the number of daily marijuana users increased 92 percent between 2001 and 2014,[53] and in 2017, the monthly use rate of marijuana was 60 percent higher than it was in 2007.[54]

Of the illicit drugs, heroin is the most addictive, with nearly 25 percent who try it becoming addicted.[55] With marijuana, approximately 10 percent of first-time users become addicted. If the person tries it more than once, that percentage increases to 15 percent.[56] As 90 percent of those who try marijuana do not become addicted, it is not surprising that so many are convinced that it cannot be addictive—a belief rejected by virtually any professional working in substance abuse.

Any comparison between outlawing narcotics and the prohibition of alcohol must account for the devastation caused by drugs. A simple recitation of the crimes related to alcohol intoxication does not account for this country's overwhelmingly greater alcohol consumption as compared to drug use. When adjusted for use rates, if one were to ingest narcotics, he or she would be several times more likely to commit a crime while impaired when compared to one who consumes a beer. While a person may have a beer during the football game, the notion of recreational intravenous heroin use is ridiculous. But much more importantly, individuals and groups just do not in any detectable way commit a multitude of crimes to support alcohol use, while the virtual entirety of drug use is supported by victimizing others both directly and indirectly. Several states have legalized marijuana, in part based on the proposition that legalizing the drug would reduce the crime associated with the illegality. However, as illustrated in the previous chapter, quite the opposite took place.

The attempted comparisons of early twentieth-century alcohol use with modern-day addictive narcotics are flawed at every level. This nation has a well-delineated history regarding the impacts of legalizing versus prohibiting drug use, as well as a track record of enforcing those laws versus declining to do so. One would think that proponents of narcotic legalization and regulation under the supervision of medical professionals would at least wait a decade past the opioid overdose epidemic (the consequence of vast numbers of prescriptions written for pain medication) to argue that such a plan is a safe solution to drug use. It's no wonder legalization advocates hang their hat on laws targeting alcohol nearly a century ago—the more recent historical record offers them nothing but facts inconsistent with their narrative.

8

The Lack of Alternatives

The discussion of criminal justice reform has been dominated by the promotion of alternatives to incarceration and enforcement. Jeffrey Stamm has observed that the proponents of drug legalization "appear to have succeeded in reshaping public opinion toward the belief that only therapeutic—not legal—measures are the permissible answer."[1] To be sure, within the last twenty-five years, the criminal justice system has completely morphed from navigating the legal paradigm to prove whether someone committed a prohibited act and assess punishment to the largest social science project in our nation's history. As Thomas Sowell observed in his persuasive book *Intellectuals in Society,* intellectuals who have never run a business have been remarkedly confident that they know which businesses are being run incorrectly.[2] Likewise, despite the purported wisdom of the intellectual and academic class relating to criminal justice, the police officers and prosecutors who dedicate their lives to the protection of the public have an incalculable amount of information on criminals, and career police officers and prosecutors are nearly unanimous in rejecting both the premises and promised outcomes of criminal justice reform mandates. A recurring theme throughout Sowell's book is the truism that intellectuals dismiss firsthand knowledge in favor of abstract ideas. Not only are the experience and wisdom of those who have dedicated themselves to protecting the public an inspiration for this book but it is my hope to convey some of that knowledge so that we all may live in a safer, more prosperous society.

The Allure of Rehab

When it comes to drug crimes, advocates for reform often juxtapose the cost of incarceration against the cost of drug treatment. For instance, just one position paper advocating for increased drug treatment in lieu of incarceration, titled "Drug Rehab Instead of Prison Could Save Billions," has as its lead tenet that "initial drug treatment is less expensive than incarceration."[3] But these sound bites deserve careful examination. Criminal justice reform is filled with seemingly clear terms, but those words are subject to very malleable uses. First of all, what exactly is "drug treatment," and just how does one claim that drug treatment "works"? The American Addiction Center, a group dedicated to treating the drug user, identifies the problem within the drug treatment community as follows:

> There is no standard definition of rehab, so there is no standardized way to measure the success of addiction centers. Many base their success rates on unreliable metrics, such as completion of the program, sobriety rates immediately after treatment, client interviews, [or] internal studies.[4]

Clearly the discussion regarding drug offenders and treatment has been presented to the public as an oversimplified binary choice, and a financial one at that: the cost of incarceration versus the cost of drug treatment. And virtually every such presentation of the false binary choice carries with it the assumption that drug treatment "works" as a foregone conclusion. In much the same manner that Hayek stated that propaganda for socialism utilizes changing the definition of simple words, the definition of success for drug addiction actually includes failure. Asserting that relapse (a euphemism for both recurrent drug use and the contemporaneous property and violent crime supporting it) is part of the "disease" in reality makes the evaluation of drug treatment programs completely elusive. In fact, the U.S. government has a web page titled "How Effective Is Drug Abuse Treatment?," which states the following:

> Unfortunately, when relapse occurs many deem treatment a failure. This is not the case: Successful treatment for addiction typically requires continual evaluation and modification as appropriate, similar to the approach taken for other chronic diseases.[5]

Not surprisingly, the document has the following words emphasized in a pull quote: "Relapse rates for addiction resemble those of other chronic diseases such as diabetes, hypertension, and asthma."[6] This document spans several paragraphs and contains well in excess of three hundred words. However, the U.S. government, through its National Institute on Drug Abuse, never attempts to answer the question it posed. The document is completely devoid of even an attempt to advise the reader just how often drug treatment fails and completely eliminates expectations by asserting that failure does not constitute failure.

Sowell has recognized that intellectuals tend to conceptualize ideas as abstract people in an abstract world, which is markedly different from the realities of flesh-and-blood people in the real world.[7] The vast difference between how social scientists define success and failure for drug treatment compared to reality can be illustrated by the following scenario. Suppose the mother of a heroin-addicted son spends tens of thousands of dollars putting her son into an inpatient drug program. Within weeks of his release, he again uses heroin, leading to a fatal overdose. If anyone were to ask that mother if her son's drug treatment "worked," no doubt this forever grieving parent would respond in a firm negative. However, under the standards of the treatment community at large and the National Institute on Drug Abuse, the inpatient treatment did not fail. In the abstract, it is quite easy for an advocacy group to claim "when relapse occurs many deem treatment a failure. This is not the case." But when the word *relapse* is used as a euphemism for a fatal overdose or even a drug-motivated crime, those of us in the real world have quite a different take.

Suppose one hundred people enroll in a drug treatment program. Exactly how will that program report its success thereafter? While this may be a good question, it has no good answer. The program may only count those who complete the program or complete the program and continue with aftercare, and even if the program is only counting those who finish aftercare while not acknowledging those who fell out, how is sobriety actually determined? The success could be counted by simple self-reporting of the addict or perhaps the lack of arrest after a specific interval of time. Some industry professionals assert quite promising rates of success, but these success rates typically reflect those who complete treatment. As 70–80 percent of people drop out of drug treatment within three to six months, such success rates are not nearly as encouraging as advertised.[8]

While the exact definition of what constitutes success in drug treatment may be elusive, there are some data regarding the number of times drug addicts enter treatment. For instance, a University of Boston study found that the mean number of times people enter drug treatment before treatment takes is 6.9.[9] Other studies put the average number of times somewhere around five.[10] To further complicate the evaluative process, some advocacy groups acknowledge that on average, a drug user will attempt more than five treatment programs prior to attaining sobriety but point out that the median number is closer to two. That is, about half of those seeking drug treatment require only two treatment attempts prior to attaining some manner of sustained sobriety, and the remaining half of drug users entering treatment need two or more. Therefore, treatment advocates argue, the median is a better gauge of treatment success, as nearly half the drug user population experiences success in two or fewer attempts. While that may be a convenient measure within the academic and social science world, that leaves the remaining half of the drug user population attempting drug treatment and failing in excess of eight to twelve times, depending which research "average" one uses. And those individuals, who are in and out of drug treatment, victimizing our society along the way, are the precise individuals the police officers and prosecutors deal with each and every day. Portraying drug treatment as a panacea for the vast majority of drug addicts (and the consequent crimes against person and property) fails at just about every level of analysis.

Some argue that there are tiers of addiction and that an addict's potential success is dependent on the marrying up of the particular addict's level of addiction with the appropriate program, thereby further complicating generic assertions of effectiveness.[11] There is yet another concept in the addiction world known as spontaneous recovery, by which an addict appears simply to stop the substance abuse by some combination of will power, bottoming out, or some life-changing event.[12] Although the research on spontaneous recovery may be scarce, and the studies that exist are not large scale, its existence does demonstrate that some people just quit using drugs—and quit committing both the crimes financing drug use and the crimes of violence committed while impaired by narcotics.

To be sure, those addicted to drugs should seek drug treatment, but drug treatment successes in reality are akin to dieting programs for weight loss. The spouse of an obese individual can buy low-fat cupcakes or sugar-free pudding for the pantry, but until that individual commits to a lifestyle change, every dietary program is doomed to failure. To that end, the notion that drug rehabilitation programs are in any way a substitute for the existence and enforcement of laws prohibiting the distribution and use of addictive psychoactive narcotics cannot be reconciled with the reality of our experience with decades of drug treatment. If these programs themselves cannot clearly define success, then the programs cannot clearly be deemed successful.

The Cost of Rehab

While the range of what treatment "costs" is wide, one should not in any way think that drug rehabilitation programs are inexpensive. A simple outpatient detox can cost $1,500, and a thirty-day inpatient program can cost from $6,000 to $30,000, while a ninety-day inpatient program can cost up to $60,000. In fact, in 2019, our nation spent nearly $37 billion on drug treatment.[13]

The billions spent on drug treatment are overwhelming funded by the government or private insurance (with those costs passed on through raised premiums to other insureds). Perhaps an independent evaluation of the efficacy of such programs consuming eleven-figure sums would be in order. To be sure, those who promote treatment in lieu of punishment tend to profit when such programs are mandated by the criminal justice system. The unfortunate reality is that any effort to promote drug treatment as cheap, especially compared to incarceration, would be shrouded in the propaganda techniques outlined throughout this book.

The Disease Model

As has been shown from statements of the National Institute on Drug Abuse, drug addiction has been characterized as a disease and analogized to other ailments, such as heart disease or diabetes. In casting doubt on the disease model, James Q. Wilson has noted that while food and nicotine also are addictive, the abuse of those compounds is viewed as a social shortcoming rather than an analogy to chronic disease.[14] To further illustrate the point, at a time when estimates showed 25 percent of Chinese males were opium dependent, the totalitarian Mao decreed that drug use and drug addiction would be punishable by death, with many executions actually being carried out. Within three years of Mao's decree, China had virtually solved its drug problem.[15] While such action is unconscionable, would similar decrees by a dictator result in cures for diabetes or cancer? Clearly the point is not that capital punishment for drug use is an effective option but rather that drug addiction is not similar to diabetes or cancer.

While a relapse oftentimes results in fatal overdose, a fatal drug overdose in a jail or prison is virtually unheard of. Drug treatment advocates are fond of comparing drug treatment to cancer treatment. The analogy states that if one attempts radiation and chemotherapy only for the cancer to subsequently return, a rational person would engage in radiation and chemotherapy again in the hope that such measures would work the second time—and unsuccessful drug treatment should be evaluated in the same fashion. However, if medical professionals had another treatment option which resulted in 99.999 percent of cancer patients surviving the disease (such as the complete absence of fatal overdose while incarcerated), wouldn't that treatment option be lauded and promoted by the medical community? The preceding examples illustrate just a few of the many shortcomings of the disease model. Will those advocating criminal justice reform at least acknowledge that more addicts fatally overdose in drug treatment than overdose while incarcerated? Do not hold your breath waiting for any consistency in the application of the disease model.

Programs in Prison

Common sense dictates that if the successful treatment program is hard to find in society, programs administered in prison would fare no better. In her book *The War on Cops*, Heather MacDonald outlined the shortcomings of prison programs aimed at rehabilitating offenders and found that "the proof that 'evidence-based treatment' can [prevent crime on the streets] is not there, at least not yet."[16] In fact, MacDonald determined that none of the six prison reentry programs evaluated by the Department of Justice was found to be effective.[17] Importantly, MacDonald pointed out that in 2012, Joan Petersilla, a member of the National Institute of Justice, a group that openly advocates for alternatives to incarceration, commented on prison rehabilitation programs by stating that researchers "don't have the models, we can't replicate them, and if we can't replicate them, we can't scale them up."[18]

Again, if the private sector has fallen short of effectively combating deviance and drug addiction, any skeptic of big government would be hard-pressed to believe that bureaucracies could accomplish what private enterprise cannot. The harsh reality is this: any person who finds himself or herself in prison for a drug or property crime in modern-day America has almost certainly had ample opportunities for or stints in alternative programs and evidence-based community therapy and most certainly was not unfamiliar with the local jails or court systems prior to incarceration. Despite the popularity of notions of rehabilitation, the pervasive presence of treatment facilities, and the existence of more "rehabilitative" programs than ever, prisoner recidivism is astronomically high. The largest study of prisoner recidivism in history, more than four hundred thousand prisoners released from thirty states, found that on average, a person released from prison is arrested five times. In fact, nearly half were arrested within the first year of release, and 83 percent were arrested during the nine-year research period.[19] Put simply, our nation is releasing more and more prisoners, and crime continues to increase, notably by those being released.

Alternatives in Court

The American court system within the last twenty-five years has fundamentally transformed from its historical role. The impact of social science and its multitude of theories on prosecutions and the judiciary has been that the modern-day criminal courtroom is nearly unrecognizable.

In fact, over the last generation, America has looked to the court system to address virtually every perceived shortcoming in society. No longer is prosecuting an offender merely about proving he or she committed an unlawful act and doling out punishment, but the court system is largely a social service system implementing a number of programs, many of which have developed into special interest groups. In fact, the American criminal justice system has become the single biggest social rehabilitation program in world history. And even if one were to believe in the effectiveness of this fundamental transformation of the court system into the therapeutic paradigm, prosecutors, judges, and defense attorneys have absolutely no training in these social sciences. Sowell has noted that the intellectual movement seeking social change through the criminal justice system necessarily involves lawyers and judges making decisions in areas far outside their expertise—which by definition will be amateur decisions.[20] Prosecutors receive advanced degrees, doctoral degrees in fact, in the practice of law. The application of the law entails the presentation of evidence to persuade a finder of fact to determine whether a certain allegation is true. The attorneys on each side, in an adversarial setting, navigate the codes and procedures in their attempt to persuade the trier of fact. Judges are to be arbiters of the law who oversee this adversarial, fact-finding proceeding.

In a far cry from the traditional and historical role of the courtroom, these therapeutic programs permeate virtually every aspect of the criminal justice process. A modern-day courtroom comprises programs such as drug court, DUI court, veterans court, mental health court, community sentencing, drug and alcohol evaluations, court services, parenting classes, impact panels, batterers assessment, and substance abuse counseling, along with innumerable acronyms denoting other programs or social science assessments. Compounding the problem is that criminals can, and often do, fake the results of psychological tests quite easily.[21] These compulsory efforts dominate the time and attention of the officers of the court, and many of these programs are funded at taxpayer expense or are mandated assessments the offender is ordered to pay.

In her book, MacDonald notes that one of the most promising methods of dealing with criminal offenders is known as SAC (for "swift and certain"), the results of which indicate that even more moderate punishments have a future deterrent effect so long as those punishments are implemented quickly and without exception.[22] In fact, alternative court programs, such as drug court, that boast substantial success rates do impose sanctions quickly, regardless of the excuses for program violations.

However, the modern-day criminal docket shows anything but quick and adequate punishments for most offenses other than murder and sex crimes, and punishments are neither certain nor consistent. Virtually any habitual substance abuser who has hurt society, including those closest to the offender, is surrounded by an enabler, a well-meaning family member who wants to understand and support the offender, but these efforts in reality have made the situation worse—actually empowering the addiction. It is high time our nation realizes that the criminal justice system's lax enforcement (from decriminalizing to lack of prosecution and crowded dockets) is an absolute enabler for drug and property crime. The decades of social engineering for offenders have produced nothing but a higher number of offenders as well as a higher number of incidents of offense for these offenders before they are effectively punished by incarceration.

To be sure, prosecutors, judges, and defense attorneys have not asked to become social workers, but such programs were the product of legislative efforts of advocacy groups. In an aggravating bit of irony, the new generation of social advocates has cited overcrowded dockets as an indication of overzealous charging by prosecutors. However, just a few decades ago, domestic abuse and driving under the influence were prosecuted primarily in municipal courts, protective orders did not exist, threats of violence and stalking were not illegal, the lack of child abuse hearsay laws prohibited many child abuse prosecutions, forensic interviews of children were yet to be a discipline, a high school student above the age of consent engaged in consensual sex with a teacher was not unlawful—but amendments to our laws have placed these acts into the purview of state and county courts. This is not to say that any of the preceding changes were ill advised but rather to demonstrate that a simple statistical analysis of prosecution numbers from decades before to assess charging decisions is a silly exercise, but one modern-day court critics use to advocate in support of their latest theory. And to make matters worse, these efforts at making the justice system a therapeutic environment have strained the resources of the entire system—in fact, these programs have come at a cost: the resources and focus of an overburdened court system. Regardless of the good intentions motivating this structural shift in the criminal justice system, one must ask whether these burdensome requirements placed on all personnel within the judicial system have produced results worth the cost.

The Role of Psychotherapy
(and a Look at the Psychopath)

Surrounding the overall premise of alternatives is that virtually all of these ideas are in one way or another psychotherapy—"social science." Dr. Robert Hare's work has been highlighted in this book already, and his creation of the psychopathy checklist to diagnose psychopaths was chronicled in his book *Without Conscience—the Disturbing World of Psychopaths among Us*. Police officers, prosecutors, judges, probation officers, court services personnel, treatment specialists, or anyone who deals with repeat offenders should not just read Hare's book but keep a copy at his or her desk as reference material to be reviewed often.

Hare wrote his profound book in 1993, but his enlightenment regarding the application of psychotherapy to criminal offenders provides crucial insight into contemporary criminal justice reform movements. Earlier, in chapter 5, I devoted an entire section to showing how flawed presumptions completely undermine the efficacy of reform efforts (both in wealth redistribution and criminal justice reform). Hare makes the point that the word *treatment* necessarily presumes that there is something to treat, and psychopaths do not think there is any defect in their actions.[23] Whatever the percentage of habitual offenders who sincerely believe they need to change, it is small indeed.

In the book, Hare notes that there are at least 2 million psychopaths in North America.[24] Interestingly enough, that is roughly the number of individuals incarcerated in the United States. While the preceding certainly does not at all mean that all prisoners are psychopaths, Hare's observations regarding the application of psychotherapy to a psychopath is certainly instructive in light of current efforts to transform the criminal justice system into the therapeutic paradigm. Regarding the overall state of social science, Hare said,

Attachment theories continue to be popular in large part because they appear to "explain" everything from anxiety and depression to multiple personality disorder, schizophrenia, eating disorders, alcoholism, and crime. But most empirical support from these theories comes from retrospective reports of early experiences, certainly not the most reliable sources of scientific data.[25]

In fact, Hare's book has an entire section explaining why treatment is ineffective for psychopaths. The following are the reasons Hare outlines to show treatment does not work for psychopaths:

1. A psychopath's pattern of behavior and attitudes are well entrenched by the time he or she makes a first attempt at formal treatment.
2. A psychopath is oftentimes protected from the negative repercussions of his or her behaviors by well-meaning family members (i.e., the enablers).
3. Psychopaths do not seek treatment on their own.
4. Once in a therapeutic setting, a psychopath typically simply goes "through the motions."
5. A psychopath will typically view a therapeutic program as a rationalization or excuse for his or her behavior while also learning about the human vulnerability he or she seeks to exploit.
6. In these group and individual programs, a psychopath will often dominate the sessions, sometimes controlling the topics of discussion.[26]

This book makes no effort to put forth some global diagnosis of psychopathy onto habitual criminals, but it is without question that at least the first five of the preceding reasons would apply to the overwhelming majority of repeat drug and property offenders. If the presence of these factors dooms efforts to change the behavior of a psychopath, why would these factors not also seriously inhibit the treatment of any other habitual offender? It should not be surprising that police officers and prosecutors have little faith in the ability of therapy to correct the deviance of outlaws, and this skepticism is not due to a distrust of the disciplines promoting therapy in lieu of enforcement. Rather, police officers and prosecutors have had front row seats in these efforts to mandate therapy onto criminals and witnessed not just a lack of effectiveness but the serious inhibiting of the public safety mission.

Regarding the popularity of professionals claiming they can treat psychopathy, Hare said,

> Despite the hundreds of attempts to treat these individuals and the great variety of techniques tried, there have been few programs that meet acceptable scientific and methodological standards.... Most of what we know is based primarily on clinical folklore, single-case studies, poor diagnostic and methodological procedures, and inadequate program evaluation.[27]

As we have shown, the drug rehabilitation and therapeutic programs in prison have fared no better. Unfortunately, despite the use of quasi-scientific terms and impressive acronyms, the social sciences simply have not mastered the knowledge of human deviance in the same manner that quantum physicists explain the molecule. While microbiologists have decoded DNA, sociologists simply have not decoded the human personality. In the epilogue to his book, Hare states,

> The criminal justice system spends billions of dollars every year in a vain attempt to "rehabilitate" or "resocialize" psychopaths *and other persistent offenders.* But these terms—popular with politicians and prison administrators—are little more than buzz words.[28]

The deviant human has existed for millennia, and even societies preceding recorded history created rules and consequences for protecting themselves from these internal threats. It would be comforting if the social science disciplines could effectively diagnose and treat the outlaw as a physician treats high blood pressure.

The entire criminal justice system has completely deviated from its historical core purpose toward this therapeutic model—the effort has produced little verifiable success, and no one can seriously contest that we have all taken our eye off the ball. The success of enforcement at every level has been documented throughout this book.

We have examined just why many conservatives have honestly come to question enforcement and even the existence of drug laws. The foundations of libertarian philosophy need not be disturbed to make the case for drug laws and the like, but a historical examination of enforcement and the lack thereof clearly shows that the enforcement of drug laws is fundamental to small-government beliefs. The brilliant economists who exposed the propaganda promoting socialist ideals would certainly recognize the identical playbook used by antiestablishment leftists promoting the decriminalization of our public safety laws. In fact, when enforcement is measured against the historical record, the exposed propaganda, and the alternatives, well, *the prosecution rests.*

Conclusion
The Decline Is Accelerating

I began writing this book in fall 2019, but I had no idea what was about to come. George Floyd was arrested after he was reported to have attempted to pass counterfeit money at a Minneapolis business. During the arrest, a struggle ensued, and a Minneapolis police officer pinned Floyd down with a knee across his neck for several minutes, with Floyd saying he could not breathe. The exact cause of Floyd's death is still in dispute (while the police "restraint" was found to be a contributing factor, apparently the autopsy revealed no evidence of mechanical asphyxiation, and the medical examiner reportedly said that Floyd's toxicology report showed he had a "fatal level of fentanyl under normal circumstances" and that "if he were found dead at home alone and no other apparent causes, this could be acceptable to call an OD").[1] But the cell phone video of his arrest resulted in riots as well as politicians and public figures tripping over one another to make statements to prove their "wokeness."

And then the Black Lives Matter movement rose to national prominence. Secretary of Housing and Urban Development Dr. Ben Carson cautioned Americans not to confuse a slogan purportedly to support racial equality with an organization rife in profound Marxist influences.[2]

Just one prominent leader within the Black Lives Matter movement stated on national television,

> If this country doesn't give us what we want, then we will burn down this system and replace it. All right? And I could be speaking . . . figuratively. I could be speaking literally. It's a matter of interpretation.[3]

The outlandish claims were not challenged by the "mainstream" institutions, as virtually everyone appeared to be in support of the Black Lives Matter movement. The entire nation appeared verbally paralyzed and unable to confront such dangerous rhetoric, perhaps for fear of being labeled racist, privileged, or unsympathetic to the force done upon George Floyd. More than seventy years ago, Frederick Hayek noted that when the "apparatus" on the left promoted socialism, those who were not in agreement needed to be silenced and that public statements contrary to the prevailing narrative needed to be suppressed, as such dissent tended to weaken public support for the ordained vision.[4] John Stewart Mill warned of the dangers to liberty when the free exchange of ideas is curtailed.[5] It appears as if the parallels cited throughout this book continue with alarming consistency.

The next offspring of the national dysfunction was a movement to "defund the police." The city council of Minneapolis went so far as to vote to abolish the police department. In lockstep with the defund the police movement, several cities (invariably in liberal strongholds) voted to drastically cut police budgets and redirect funds to social programs.

Many national politicians on the left were in a difficult position. They could not join the calls to defund the police, as such notions were very unpopular with the general electorate, but these politicians could not criticize these movements, as their nutty members would account for part of the votes needed for a patch quilt coalition during an election year. So, America largely experienced silence from political leaders and the typical cultural loudmouths. With liberal cities experiencing rioting and lawlessness, the entire Democratic National Convention never once mentioned rioting, lawlessness, looting, destruction, or violence. It was not until after the convention (apparently after Democratic research showed that the left's silence was hurting polling numbers) that Joe Biden finally made the following statement: "The needless violence won't heal us."[6] It was a little weak, and a lot late.

The Case of Jacob Blake

Perhaps the latter part of 2020 is best represented with the case of one Jacob Blake. Blake was shot by police in Kenosha, Wisconsin, on August 23, 2020.

Initial Version

The early narrative regarding the shooting of Jacob Blake indicated that he was shot in the back as he tried to get into his car, with his three children watching in horror. Blake was reported to have previously exited his vehicle to break up a fight between two women. The situation was almost invariably described in the media as a black man shot in back by a white police officer. Some claimed that the cell phone video of the interaction between the police and Blake had captured audio with the police making references to a knife. Public officials initially declined to elaborate on whether Blake was armed. Violent demonstrations in Wisconsin followed almost immediately, and the typical pop culture figures and politicians expressed outrage.

The NBA Responds

The NBA canceled all of its games on Wednesday, August 26, 2020. Milwaukee Bucks player George Hill said, "We are calling for justice for Jacob Blake and demand the officers be held accountable."[7] On Twitter, NBA superstar LeBron James said, "And y'all wonder why we say what we say about the Police!! Someone please tell me WTF is this???!!! Exactly another black man being targeted."[8] James went on to say, "This shit is so wrong and so sad!! Feel so sorry for him, his family and OUR PEOPLE!! We want JUSTICE."

Quite notably, shortly after the NBA canceled its games, the Wisconsin Department of Justice, the agency charged with investigating the shooting, issued a public statement regarding the shooting that included the following new information:

> During the investigation following the initial incident, Mr. Blake admitted that he had a knife in his possession. DCI agents recovered a knife from the driver's side floorboard of Mr. Blake's vehicle. A search of the vehicle located no additional weapons.

Remarkably, the NBA halted its protest the following day, and playoff games resumed in full. The only action by public officials between the protest cancelations and the announcement of full resumption of games was the statement by the Wisconsin Department of Justice.

More Facts Come to Light

On the date of the shooting, Jacob Blake had a warrant out for his arrest for felony sexual assault. The *New York Post* obtained a copy of the complaint that led to Blake's warrant and some of the shocking quotations from the victim that Blake sexually assaulted her by penetrating her with his finger and, after doing so, smelled his finger and said, "Smells like you've been with other men." The victim described Blake's sexual assault as "penetrating her digitally caused her pain and humiliation and was done without her consent," while also telling the police she was "very humiliated and upset by the sexual assault." In alleging a consistent pattern of abuse by Blake, the victim also said that during her eight years of association with Blake, he would physically assault her approximately twice a year, "when he drinks heavily."[9]

Blake, who was prohibited from being at the house of his victim, showed up, prompting a 911 call to police. This is what led police to come into contact with Blake, not the police misunderstanding his good Samaritan efforts at breaking up a fight. The union representing the officer stated that Blake fought with officers trying to arrest him for his felony sexual assault charges, even putting one officer in a headlock. The shooting only took place after attempts to subdue Blake with a stun gun failed. The union representative also said,

> Mr. Blake was not unarmed. He was armed with a knife. The officers did not see the knife initially. The officers issued repeated commands for Mr. Blake to drop the knife. He did not comply.[10]

Politicians Respond

To compile all of the comments from politicians and talking heads on the Blake matter would be too arduous a task. Perhaps just the leading candidates for the office of the U.S. presidency will suffice. Presidential candidate Joe Biden said, "I do think there's a minimum need to be charged, the officers."[11] Kamala Harris, Biden's running mate, said she was "proud" of Jacob Blake. Perhaps she had expended all of her outrage relating to men accused of sexually assaulting women during the Brett Cavanaugh confirmation hearings.

Updated Summary

Jacob Blake was accused of violently committing a sexual assault on an innocent victim. A warrant was issued for his arrest; he showed up at the residence of his victim, who called 911; the police responded and tried to arrest Blake for his felony sexual assault warrant; and he fought the officers, putting one in a headlock. Officers attempted to tase Blake to no avail. He was armed with a knife and refused commands regarding the knife, and he was ultimately shot. Blake admitted that he was in possession of a knife, and in the exact place he was shot, investigators found a knife.

Current Status

At the close of 2020, there appear to be no substantive updates on the Jacob Blake case. It is as if it never was. Perhaps the real facts surrounding the Jacob Blake incident are inconvenient to the narratives pushed by those with agendas. But the damage has already been done. Have we seen any mea culpas from the public figures, media, or sports icons for the horrendously inaccurate statements made about the Kenosha officers? Not a one.

In light of what we know now, does Joe Biden think the officers need to be charged at a "minimum"? Will Biden direct his Department of Justice to indict the officers regardless of the results of the investigation? Is Kamala Harris still "proud" of Blake? Does George Hill still "demand justice for Jacob Blake"? Does LeBron James still think Jacob Blake is "another black man being targeted"?

Police oftentimes have to make quick decisions with incomplete information in rapidly evolving, stressful situations. The establishment has zero tolerance for mistakes on the part of law enforcement. But politicians, public figures, and the media complex clearly made mistaken public assertions regarding the Jacob Blake shooting.

How much each individual inaccurate public statement contributed to the violence and destruction is impossible to tabulate—without question, the collective false narratives contained in repeated misstatements led to extreme damage to person and property. Will these people atone or admit a damaging rush to judgment? Perhaps—when hell freezes over.

The Current Enforcement Experience

In the latter part of 2020, police were targeted by everyone. It was absolutely unacceptable for anyone to speak out against the Black Lives Matter movement or what the movement demanded. It did not matter that the group's title was not representative of its objectives. Congress held hearings, and everyone had something to say. Republicans and Democrats alike, most of whom had been elected for decades, raced to hold the next hearing or spout off a focus group–approved sound bite. They never once apologized for their lack of action before.

So, what happened in these cities that did not support law enforcement? Were the results as would have been predicted by the writing of this book? Homicide rate increases of 28 percent in Philadelphia and 24 percent in Portland appear to be the best-performing locales, as Minneapolis saw a 60 percent increase in homicides, New York City experienced a 130 percent increase in shootings, Chicago hit a sixty-year high in homicides, and Seattle saw over a 500 percent increase in crime.[12] These examples are not outliers—in fact, at the publication of this book, dramatic and alarming increases in violent crimes are commonplace in many cities across the United States, especially where the aforementioned charlatans were most active.

Why Do We Do What We Do?

It was already very challenging to be a member of law enforcement. If a police officer does his or her job, a trained advocate with a doctoral degree in the practice of law is waiting to attack the officer's performance, skill, or even integrity. Cottage industries are aimed at attacking the efforts of police. Absolutely no public servant encounters similar adversities. Would society tolerate intense attacks on teachers simply because teachers gave students their earned grades? Police officers are sued frequently and routinely—similar lawsuits are not faced by elected leaders, judges, attorneys, teachers, child welfare workers, counselors, or those in any other public service occupation. And the preceding landscape for law enforcement existed long before the contemporary political climate. The all-time low morale of law enforcement cannot be captured by words. Those in law enforcement ask themselves, now more than ever before, *Why do we do what we do?* Although I have had the members of public safety in mind as I wrote this book, I intended the writing to be for a general audience. But in this last section, I want to speak directly to the men and women of law enforcement.

It was a typical May afternoon in Tulsa, and a beautiful eight-year-old girl was having fun on the playground of the apartment complex where she lived with her family. But in broad daylight, a despicable man named Michael Slatton abducted her and sped away in his vehicle. I was attached to the U.S. Marshal Violent Crimes Task Force, and we were activated, along with every other available law enforcement asset. At that time, law enforcement only had a vehicle description. Earlier in the day, this registered sex offender, high on drugs, was attempting to buy coloring books at a Tulsa discount store. The alert clerk called the suburban town on his identification to advise them of his strange behavior. Because of a savvy dispatcher and good detective work, officers discovered that this sex offender drove the same type of car observed by witnesses, and Slatton's mother told officers she had not seen him for several hours. Law enforcement now had a suspect. Nearly forty miles away, a police officer had attempted to arrest an individual for public intoxication of narcotics at a fast-food restaurant. The man fought the officer, dragging him with his vehicle and injuring the officer, but the officer could identify Slatton as the suspect he had just fought. As police officers swarmed to the area, it was well after midnight and several hours after the abduction. Ultimately, a police helicopter flushed out Slatton's vehicle, and a pursuit followed. At the end of the pursuit, the little girl was not in the vehicle. Officers combed the area, ultimately finding her concealed in a tree line, her underwear tied around her neck—but alive. Slatton had no intention of leaving a witness, but the effort and skill of public safety experts ended his terror before he did worse.

Slatton had committed unspeakable crimes against this eight-year-old angel. In the following court process, this monster stayed true to form, assaulting and injuring a prosecutor before the jury, fighting with detention officers to avoid court, even changing his appearance in an attempt to thwart identification by the victim. But this brave little girl went to court, described the horrible things the disgusting man had done to her, and pointed him out to the jury. Slatton was sentenced to 120 years in prison. This story contains a lot of heroism, none more inspiring than this little girl's. Since that time, this heroine has written a book to help others victimized, has done media interviews to help victims, and has said when she grows up, she would like to be a legislator or prosecutor. During the writing of this book, this young lady was recognized for her bravery by a law enforcement association. The following day, she posted the following statement on her social media account:

> This was the best day ever! I thank every single person
> that came and helped on my case! I love you all. I am

honored to have this award. I am so glad I had a chance
to see the people that I haven't seen in a while and that
I missed so much. I couldn't be happier. This means so
much to me. Thank you all for this day.

That's why we do what we do. There are many more
Michael Slattons in the world. There are deviants and
outlaws everywhere who simply want more opportunities
to victimize the vulnerable. Nothing stands between them
and the innocent but us—and we cannot abandon them.
This book has chronicled the impact of enforcement and,
more importantly, the disasters that follow curtailing the
efforts of police officers and prosecutors. It's never been
harder to be in law enforcement, but it's never been more
important.

Notes

Introduction
1. Thomas Sowell, *Intellectuals and Society* (Basic Books, 2009), 2–3.

Chapter 2
1. S. E. Frost Jr., *The Basic Teachings of the Great Philosophers* (New Home Library, 1943), 217–18.
2. Frost, 220–21.
3. Frost, 221; Thomas Sowell, *Intellectuals and Society*, Rev. and Enl. ed. (Basic Books, 2011), 61; https://en.wikipedia.org/wiki/ Laissez-faire.
4. Sowell, *Intellectuals and Society*, 2009, 95.
5. T. Z. Lavine, *From Socrates to Sartre: The Philosophic Quest* (Bantam, 1984), 186ff., 261ff.
6. John Stewart Mill, *On Liberty* (Dover, 2002), 1.
7. Mill, 65.
8. Mill, 8, 63, 79.
9. https://en.wikipedia.org/wiki/The_Road_to_Serfdom.
10. F. A. Hayek, *The Road to Serfdom*, Definitive ed. (University of Chicago Press, 2007), 8.
11. Hayek, 6–7.
12. Hayek, 67.
13. Hayek, 44.
14. Hayek, 88.
15. Hayek, 148.
16. Hayek, 149.
17. Hayek, 148.
18. Hayek, 88.

19. Hayek, 117.
20. Hayek, 6.
21. Hayek, 100–101.
22. Hayek, 101.
23. Hayek, 50.
24. Hayek, 216–17.
25. Hayek, 20.
26. Milton Friedman and Rose Friedman, *Free to Choose* (First Harvest, 1990), 3.
27. Friedman and Friedman, 4, 309.
28. Friedman and Friedman, 5.
29. Friedman and Friedman,
30. Friedman and Friedman, 29.
31. Friedman and Friedman, 27–29.
32. Friedman and Friedman, 32.
33. Friedman and Friedman, 105–6.
34. Friedman and Friedman, 145.
35. Friedman and Friedman.
36. Friedman and Friedman, 309–10.
37. Milton Friedman, *Capitalism and Freedom*, 40th Anniversary ed. (University of Chicago Press, 2002), 25.

Chapter 3

1. Frost, *Basic Teachings of the Great Philosophers*, 95.
2. Frost, 215–16.
3. Frost, 218–19.
4. https://en.wikipedia.org/wiki/John_E._Douglas.
5. Robert D. Hare, *Without Conscience: The Disturbing World of Psychopaths among Us* (Guilford Press, 1993), 41.
6. Alex Berenson, *Tell Your Children the Truth about Marijuana, Mental Illness, and Violence* (Free Press, 2020), xix, 32, 40.

Chapter 4

1. Mill, *On Liberty*, 8.
2. Friedman and Friedman, *Free to Choose*, 106.
3. Hayek, *Road to Serfdom*, 86.
4. Friedman and Friedman, *Free to Choose*, 5.

5. "Milton Friedman on Donahue—1979," YouTube video, 45:27, August 26, 2009, https://www.youtube.com/watch?v=1EwaLys3Zak.
6. "Milton Friedman on Donahue #2," YouTube video, 46:27, August 26, 2009, https://www.youtube.com/watch?v=DvNzi7tmkx0.
7. Malone v. State, 2013 OK CR 1.
8. Mill, *On Liberty,* 63.
9. Hayek, *Road to Serfdom,* 148–49.
10. Hayek.
11. Friedman and Friedman, *Free to Choose,* 32.
12. Friedman, *Capitalism and Freedom,* 33
13. "Ben Shapiro—Decriminalize Drugs?," YouTube video, 1:58, March 14, 2019, https://www.youtube.com/watch?v=xmcLGX79ccY.
14. https://www.youtube.com/results?search_query=ben+shapiro+drug+legalization+.
15. Jeffrey B. Stamm, *On Dope, Drug Enforcement and the First Policeman* (Outskirts Press, 2016), 16.
16. Stamm, 16.
17. Stam, 13; interview with Jeffrey Stamm, February 2020.
18. Stamm, 14, quoting Dr. Steven Patrick, fellow in Neonatal–Perinatal Medicine at the University of Michigan.
19. Sowell, *Intellectuals and Society,* 2009, 112, 2–3.
20. Mill, *On Liberty,* 82.
21. Mark Koba, "Copper Theft 'Like an Epidemic' Sweeping US," July 30, 2013, https://www.cnbc.com/id/100917758.
22. https://ucr.fbi.gov/crime-in-the-u.s/2017/crime-in-the-u.s.-2017/topic-pages/crime-clock.
23. https://www.hg.org/legal-articles/facts-about-shoplifting-31291.
24. *An Examination of the Relationship between Drugs and Crime in the Midwest,* Midwest HIDTA, March 2020, 6.
25. Dale Denwalt, "Fallin OKs Bills That Will Ease Prison Growth," *Oklahoman,* April 27, 2018, https://oklahoman.com/article/5592608/fallin-oks-bills-that-will-ease-prison-growth.

26. Heather MacDonald, *The War on Cops* (Encounter Books, 2016), 188.
27. Vera Institute, "Prison Spending in 2015," https://www.vera.org/publications/price-of-prisons-2015-state-spending-trends/price-of-prisons-2015-state-spending-trends/price-of-prisons-2015-state-spending-trends-prison-spending.
28. MacDonald, *War on Cops*, 223.
29. Interview with Rogers County Undersheriff Jon Sappington, April 15. 2020.
30. Stamm, *On Dope*, 74.
31. Stamm, 75.
32. "FY 2021 Budget Highlights," https://okpolicy.org/fy-2021-budget-highlights/.
33. "What America Spends on Drug Addictions," Addiction-Treatment, https://addiction-treatment.com/in-depth/what-america-spends-on-drug-addictions.
34. *An Examination of the Relationship between Drugs and Crime*, 6.
35. Heather MacDonald, "San Francisco, Hostage to the Homeless," *City Journal* [San Francisco], Autumn 2019, https://www.city-journal.org/san-francisco-homelessness.
36. MacDonald.
37. Timothy Meads, "San Francisco Homelessness Rises 17% after City Spends $300 Million Annually to Solve Problem," *Townhall,* May 18, 2019, https://townhall.com/tipsheet/timothymeads/2019/05/18/san-francisco-homeless-rises-17-after-city-spends-300-million-annually-to-solve-problem-n2546530.
38. MacDonald, "San Francisco."

Chapter 5

1. Thomas Sowell, *Basic Economics* (Basic Books, 2015), 6.
2. Friedman, *Capitalism and Freedom,* 196.
3. Sowell, *Intellectuals and Society,* 112.
4. Sowell, 2–3.
5. Sowell, 8.
6. Hayek, *Road to Serfdom,* 57.

7. Hayek, 6.
8. Sowell, *Intellectuals and Society,* 1.
9. Friedman, *Capitalism and Freedom,* 181.
10. Mariel Alper, Matthew R. Durose, and Joshua Markman, *Update on Prisoner Recidivism: A 9-Year Follow-Up Period (2005–2014),* special report (U.S. Department of Justice Office of Justice Programs, Bureau of Justice Statistics, May 2018).
11. Friedman and Friedman, *Free to Choose,* 292–93.
12. Friedman, *Capitalism and Freedom,* 143.
13. Friedman, 293, 294.
14. Sowell, *Basic Economics,* 225.
15. Sowell, 7.
16. Sowell, *Intellectuals and Society,* 291.
17. Jeffrey A. Miron and Katherine Waldock, *The Budgetary Impact of Ending Drug Prohibition* (Cato Institute, 2010), https://www.cato.org/sites/cato.org/files/pubs/pdf/DrugProhibitionWP.pdf.
18. Hayek, *Road to Serfdom,* 196.
19. Hayek, 24.
20. Friedman, *Capitalism and Freedom,* 5.
21. Sowell, *Intellectuals and Society,* 8.
22. Sowell, 157.
23. Hayek, *Road to Serfdom,* 173.
24. Hayek, 8.
25. Hayek, 184.
26. Hayek, 202.
27. Hayek, 212.
28. Sowell, *Intellectuals and Society,* 151–52.
29. Hayek, *Road to Serfdom,* 173.
30. Hayek, 8.
31. Hayek, 196.
32. Hayek, 176.
33. Bernard Goldberg, *Bias* (Regnery, 2002), 58–61.
34. Goldberg, 63, 66.
35. Goldberg, 77.
36. Berenson, *Tell Your Children the Truth,* 180–89.
37. Berenson, 94–95.

38. Berenson, 103.
39. Stamm, *On Dope,* 252.
40. Sowell, *Intellectuals and Society,* 5.
41. Sowell, 23.
42. Friedman and Friedman, *Free to Choose,* 301.
43. Hayek, *Road to Serfdom,* 171.
44. Hayek, 174.
45. Sowell, *Intellectuals and Society,* 146.
46. Thomas Sowell, "Government Statistics," YouTube video, 8:07, https://www.youtube.com/watch?v=xc3AokM_bpw.
47. Steve Lewis, "The Cost of Maintaining the World's Highest Incarceration," Oklahoma Policy Institute, September 10, 2018, https://okpolicy.org/the-cost-of-maintaining-the-w orlds-highest-incarceration-capitol-update/.
48. Chris Mai and Ram Subramanian, "The Price of Prisons," Vera Institute, May 2017, https://www.vera.org/downloads/ publications/the-price-of-prisons-2015-state-spending-trends. pdf.
49. Hayek, *Road to Serfdom,* 160.
50. Friedman, *Capitalism and Freedom,* 1.
51. Berenson, *Tell Your Children the Truth,* 67.
52. Friedman and Friedman, *Free to Choose,* 22.
53. Friedman, *Capitalism and Freedom,* 180.
54. Friedman, 181.

Chapter 6

1. Jet Akst, "The Elixir Tragedy," June 2013, https://www. the-scientist.com/foundations/the-elixir-tragedy-1937-39231.
2. Malcolm Gladwell, "Is Marijuana as Safe as We Think?," *New Yorker,* January 14, 2019, https://www.newyorker.com/ magazine/2019/01/14/is-marijuana-as-safe-as-we-think.
3. Sadie F. Dingfelder, "The First Modern Psychology Study," *Monitor,* July/August 2020, https://www.apa.org/ monitor/2010/07-08/franklin.
4. American Epilepsy Society President Michael D. Privitera, M.D., to Representative Matthew Baker of the Pennsylvania Legislature, March 11, 2016.

5. *Washington Post,* "Let's Make Sure This Crisis Doesn't Go to Waste," Washington Post, March 25, https://www. washingtonpost.com/opinions/2020/03/25/lets-make-sure-thi s-crisis-doesnt-go-waste/.

6. "Opioids: Perception of Pain," https://www.health.state.mn.us/ communities/opioids/prevention/painperception.html.

7. https://www.healthsystemtracker.org/chart-collection/u-s-life-expectancy-compare-countries/#item-start.

8. "Overdose Death Rates," National Institute on Drug Abuse, https://www.drugabuse.gov/related-topics/trends-statistics/ overdose-death-rates.

9. "Is Marijuana a Gateway Drug?," National Institute on Drug Abuse, https://www.drugabuse.gov/publications/ research-reports/marijuana/marijuana-gateway-drug; Stamm, *On Dope,* 240.

10. Berenson, *Tell Your Children the Truth,* xviii.

11. Berenson, 109–10.

12. Berenson, 113.

13. "Legalizing Marijuana Decreases Fatal Opiate Overdoses, Study Shows," American Addiction Centers, https://drugabuse. com/legalizing-marijuana-decreases-fatal-opiate-overdoses/.

14. Berenson, *Tell Your Children the Truth,* 116.

15. Berenson, 116; Gladwell, "Is Marijuana as Safe as We Think?"

16. Gabrielle Campbell, Wayne D. Hall, Amy Peacock, Nicholas Lintzeris, Raimondo Bruno, Briony Larance, Suzanne Nielsen et al., "Effect of Cannabis Use in People with Chronic Non-cancer Pain Prescribed Opioids: Findings from a 4-Year Prospective Cohort Study," *Lancet Public Health* 3, no. 7 (2018): e341–50.

17. "Marijuana, Opioids, and Pain Management," SAM, https:// learnaboutsam.org/wp-content/uploads/2018/10/9-Oct-2018-Opioid-One-Pager-briefing-print.pdf.

18. American Society of Addiction Medicine, white paper on "State-Level Proposals to Legalize Marijuana," adopted by the ASAM Board of Directors, July 25, 2012, 3–4; Stamm, *On Dope,* 240.

19. Stamm, *On Dope,* 260.

20. "Marijuana Legalization: Quick Facts," SAM, https://learnaboutsam.org/wp-content/uploads/2018/11/Oct-2018-Quick-Facts.v4.pdf; "Tracking the Money That's Legalizing Marijuana and Why It Matters," National Families in Action, 2017, https://www.nationalfamilies.org/assets/pdfs/Tracking_the_Money_Thats_Legalizing_Marijuana_and_Why_It_Matters_FINAL-R_3.15.2017-R.pdf.
21. Berenson, *Tell Your Children the Truth*, xix.
22. Berenson, 40.
23. California Proposition 215.
24. "Marijuana Legalization: Quick Facts."
25. Berenson, Tell Your Children the Truth, 148.
26. Peter Roy-Byrne, "Cannabis Use May Be Causally Related to Depression and Suicidal Ideation," *Lancet Psychiatry*, September 2017.
27. https://en.wikipedia.org/wiki/National_Academy_of_Sciences.
28. http://www.nasonline.org/membership/.
29. National Academies of Sciences, Engineering, and Medicine, *The Health Effects of Cannabis and Cannabinoids—the Current State of Evidence and Recommendations for Research* (Washington, DC: National Academies Press, January 2017).
30. National Academies of Sciences.
31. National Academies of Sciences.
32. National Academies of Sciences, 54.
33. National Academies of Sciences, 167.
34. National Academies of Sciences, xxxi.
35. National Academies of Sciences, 169.
36. National Academies of Sciences, 172.
37. National Academies of Sciences, 167.
38. National Academies of Sciences, 168.
39. National Academies of Sciences, 167–68.
40. National Academies of Sciences, 175.
41. https://en.wikipedia.org/wiki/National_Institutes_of_Health.
42. https://en.wikipedia.org/wiki/National_Institutes_of_Health.
43. NIDA Archives.
44. NIDA Archives.

45. NIDA Archives.
46. Alex Berenson, "Marijuana Is More Dangerous than You Realize," *Dallas Morning News,* January 15, 2019, https:// www.dallasnews.com/opinion/commentary/2019/01/15/ marijuana-is-more-dangerous-than-you-realize/.
47. American Society of Addiction Medicine, white paper, 14.
48. Rocky Mountain High Intensity Drug Trafficking Area (RMHIDTA), "The Legalization of Marijuana in Colorado," *The Impact* 5 (October 2017): 117.
49. RMHIDTA, 130.
50. Stamm, *On Dope,* 252–53.
51. RMHIDTA, "Legalization of Marijuana in Colorado," 39.
52. RMHIDTA, 2.
53. RMHIDTA.
54. Oregon–Idaho High Intensity Drug Trafficking Area (OIHIDTA), *An Initial Assessment of Cannabis Production, Distribution, and Consumption in Oregon 2018—an Insight Report,* 1st ed., 30.
55. OIHIDTA, 23.
56. "Lessons Learned after 4 Years of Legalization," SAM, October 2016, 4, https://www.in.gov/ipac/files/ SAM-report-on-CO-and-WA-issued-31-Oct-2016.pdf.
57. "Lessons Learned."
58. "Lessons Learned," 5–6.
59. RMHIDTA, "Legalization of Marijuana in Colorado," 3.
60. RMHIDTA, 83.
61. RMHIDTA.
62. RMHIDTA, 3.
63. RMHIDTA, 23.
64. "The Costs of Marijuana Legalization to Society," SAM, https:// learnaboutsam.org/wp-content/uploads/2018/06/14Nov2017- v5-costs-to-society.pdf.
65. "Marijuana and Insurance in the U.S.," SAM, https:// learnaboutsam.org/wp-content/uploads/2018/10/ Insurance-One-Pager.v3.pdf.
66. OIHIDTA, *An Initial Assessment,* 31.
67. OIHIDTA, 32.

68. OIHIDTA.

69. American Society of Addiction Medicine, white paper, 12.

70. OIHIDTA, *An Initial Assessment,* 33.

71. Christopher Smith, "Fatal Crashes Involving Marijuana Increase after Legalization: Study," Motor1, January 30, 2020, https://www.motor1.com/news/395995/fatal-car-crashes-marijuana-increase-study/.

72. National Institute on Drug Abuse, "Marijuana: Facts for Teens," https://teens.drugabuse.gov/national-drug-alcohol-facts-week/marijuana-facts-teens.

73. OIHIDTA, *An Initial Assessment,* 33.

74. RMHIDTA, "Legalization of Marijuana in Colorado," 13.

75. "Colorado," SAM, https://learnaboutsam.org/wp-content/uploads/2020/03/Colorado-One-Pager-39pdf.pdf.

76. RMHIDTA, "Legalization of Marijuana in Colorado," 29.

77. American Society of Addiction Medicine, white paper, 9–10.

78. "Lessons Learned," 15.

79. "Lessons Learned."

80. "Lessons Learned," 24.

81. "Lessons Learned."

82. "Lessons Learned," 25.

83. American Society of Addiction Medicine, white paper, 16.

84. "Lessons Learned," 25.

85. RMHIDTA, "Legalization of Marijuana in Colorado," 117.

86. RMHIDTA, 128.

87. Sowell, *Intellectuals and Society,* 19.

88. RMHIDTA, "Legalization of Marijuana in Colorado," 93.

89. RMHIDTA, 95.

90. RMHIDTA, 96.

91. RMHIDTA.

92. RMHIDTA, 109.

93. OIHIDTA, *An Initial Assessment,* 9.

94. OIHIDTA, 36.

95. OIHIDTA, 38–39.

96. "Lessons Learned," 26.

97. "Lessons Learned," 13.

98. "Lessons Learned," 14.

99. "Lessons Learned."

100. "Lessons Learned," 12.

101. "Lessons Learned."

102. "Revenues vs. Reality," SAM, https://learnaboutsam.org/wp-content/uploads/2020/05/Revenues-vs-Reality-0520-4.pdf.

103. American Society of Addiction Medicine, white paper, 11.

Chapter 7

1. https://starcasm.net/mug-shot-tulsa-woman-arrested-for-cooking-meth-in-a-walmart/.

2. Dr. Penny Grant, Drug Endangered Children Study, Tulsa, Oklahoma.

3. Matt Barnard and Nicole Marshall, "Two Injured in Tulsa Meth Fire, Another Arrested," *Oklahoman,* https://oklahoman.com/article/3357777/two-injured-in-tulsa-meth-fire-another-arrested.

4. "Pair Sentenced for Toddler's Death in Tulsa Meth Lab Fire," February 1, 2013, https://www.newson6.com/story/20936762/pair-sentenced-for-toddlers-death-in-north-tulsa-meth-lab-fire; "1 Acquitted, 2 Others Waive Jury Trial in Meth Lab Fire That Killed Toddler," January 25, 2013, https://www.newson6.com/story/20709528/one-found-not-guilty-two-others-waive-jury-trial-in-15-month-olds-death-in-fire.

5. Jackie DelPilar, "FOX23 Investigates: The Evolving Meth Market," January 31, 2020, https://www.fox23.com/news/fox23-investigates/fox23-investigates-evolving-meth-market/EPUYJUCSIJBMVKF6GQ7RO75VSA/.

6. Jenny L. Wiley, Julie A. Marusich, John W. Huffman, Robert L. Balster, and Brian F. Thomas, "Hijacking of Basic Research: The Case of Synthetic Cannabinoids," *Methods Report* 2011 (2011): 17971.

7. Stamm, *On Dope,* 133.

8. Stamm, 141.

9. Stamm, 141–42.

10. Stamm, 46.

11. Sowell, *Intellectuals and Society,* 28.

12. Stamm, *On Dope,* 47.

13. George L. Kelling, "How New York Became Safe: The Full Story," *City Journal,* special issue, 2019, https://www.city-journal.org/html/how-new-york-became-safe-full-story-13197.html.

14. Martin Hill Ortiz, "Violent Crime Rates under New York City Mayor Giuliani," https://martinhillortiz.blogspot.com/2016/09/violent-crime-rates-under-new-york-city.html.

15. https://www.courtinnovation.org/sites/default/files/media/document/2019/Bail_Reform_NY_Summary.pdf.

16. https://www.courtinnovation.org/sites/default/files/media/document/2019/Bail_Reform_NY_Summary.pdf.

17. Jonathan Dienst and Jon Schuppe, "As City Sees Uptick in Crime, NYC Mayor Calls for Bail Reform Adjustment," February 5, 2020, https://www.nbcnewyork.com/news/politics/as-city-sees-uptick-in-crime-nyc-mayor-calls-for-bail-reform-adjustment/2278653/.

18. Ray Carter, "Change in Felony Threshold Tied to Increased Crime," October 28, 2019, https://ocpathink.org/post/change-in-felony-threshold-tied-to-increased-crime.

19. Maureen Wurtz, "780's Unintended Consequences; Tulsa Now the Top Place for Thefts at Quik Trip Stores," February 18, 2019, https://ktul.com/news/investigations/780s-unintended-consequences-tulsa-now-the-top-place-for-thefts-at-quik-trip-stores.

20. Barbara Hoberock, "QuikTrip Questioned on Assertion That Crime at Its Stores Is Up 300% because of SQ780," *Tulsa World,* August 21, 2019, https://www.tulsaworld.com/news/quiktrip-questioned-on-assertion-that-crime-at-its-stores-is/article_8ce2780c-43a9–58ef-a887-d8da25d8b255.html.

21. https://ocpathink.org/post/change-in-felony-threshold-tied-to-increased-crime.

22. https://ocpathink.org/post/change-in-felony-threshold-tied-to-increased-crime.

23. MacDonald, *War on Cops,* 34.

24. Stamm, *On Dope,* 95.

25. Stamm.

26. MacDonald, *War on Cops,* 207.

27. Jean-Jaques Rousseau, *The Social Contract* (Penguin Books, 1968), 80.
28. Stamm, *On Dope,* 233.
29. MacDonald, *War on Cops,* 108.
30. MacDonald, 69.
31. MacDonald.
32. MacDonald, 56–57.
33. MacDonald, 55–56.
34. Kurtis Lee and James Queally, "Story So Far: Who Was Freddie Gray, and What's Next for the Police Officers Charged in His Death?," *LA Times,* April 30, 2015, https://www.latimes.com/nation/nationnow/la-na-nn-freddie-gray-story-so-far-20150430-htmlstory.html.
35. https://en.wikipedia.org/wiki/Death_of_Freddie_Gray.
36. "Number of Homicides in Baltimore in 2020 Is Pacing Ahead of Last Year's Record-Breaking Rate," June 30, 2020, https://baltimore.cbslocal.com/2020/06/03/baltimore-2020-homicide-rate-latest/.
37. Stamm, *On Dope,* 257.
38. Stamm.
39. Stamm, 240.
40. Stamm, 3.
41. Berenson, *Tell Your Children the Truth,* xxix.
42. Berenson, 5.
43. Berenson, 31.
44. Stamm, *On Dope,* 252.
45. Berenson, *Tell Your Children the Truth,* 103.
46. American Society of Addiction Medicine, white paper.
47. Stamm, *On Dope,* 6.
48. Stamm, 64.
49. Dr. Kevin Sabet, keynote address to Association of Oklahoma Narcotic Enforcers Summer Conference, Catoosa, OK, August 2019.
50. Berenson, *Tell Your Children the Truth,* 167.
51. Berenson, xix.
52. OIHIDTA, *An Initial Assessment,* 10.
53. Alejandro Azofeifa, Margaret E. Mattson, Gillian Schauer, Tim

McAfee, Althea Grant, and Rob Lyerla, "National Estimates of Marijuana Use and Related Indicators—National Survey on Drug Use and Health, United States, 2002–2014," *Morbidity and Mortality Weekly Report* 65, no. 11 (2016): 1–25, https://www.cdc.gov/mmwr/volumes/65/ss/ss6511a1.htm.

54. Berenson, *Tell Your Children the Truth*, xix.
55. "Statistics on Addiction in America," Addiction Center, https://www.addictioncenter.com/addiction/addiction-statistics/.
56. Berenson, *Tell Your Children the Truth*, 137.

Chapter 8

1. Stamm, *On Dope*, 55.
2. Sowell, *Intellectuals and Society*, 62.
3. "Drug Rehab Instead of Prison Could Save Billions," Foundations Recovery Network, https://dualdiagnosis.org/drug-rehab-instead-of-prison-could-save-billions-says-report-2/.
4. "Rehab Success Rates and Statistics," American Addiction Centers, https://americanaddictioncenters.org/rehab-guide/success-rates-and-statistics.
5. "How Effective Is Drug Addiction Treatment?," National Institute on Drug Abuse, https://www.drugabuse.gov/publications/principles-drug-addiction-treatment-research-based-guide-third-edition/frequently-asked-questions/how-effective-drug-addiction-treatment.
6. "How Effective Is Drug Addiction Treatment?"
7. Sowell, *Intellectuals and Society*, 112.
8. "Rehab Success Rates and Statistics."
9. Stamm, *On Dope*, 190.
10. John F. Kelly, Martha Claire Greene, Brandon G. Bergman, William L. White, and Bettina B. Hoeppner, "How Many Recovery Attempts Does It Take to Successfully Resolve an Alcohol or Drug Problem? Estimates and Correlates from a National Study of Recovering U.S. Adults," *Alcoholism: Clinical and Experimental Research* 43, no. 7 (2019): 1533–1544, https://www.ncbi.nlm.nih.gov/pubmed/31090945.
11. "Rehab Success Rates and Statistics."

12. "Rehab Success Rates and Statistics."
13. "Total Federal Drug Control Spending in the United States from FY 2012 to FY 2021," https://www.statista.com/statistics/618857/total-federal-drug-control-spending-in-us/.
14. Stamm, *On Dope*, 29–30.
15. Stamm, 197.
16. MacDonald, *War on Cops*, 208.
17. MacDonald, 219.
18. MacDonald, 208.
19. Alper, Durose, and Markman, *Update on Prisoner Recidivism*.
20. Sowell, *Intellectuals and Society*, 25.
21. Hare, *Without Conscience*, 31.
22. MacDonald, *War on Cops*, 226.
23. Hare, *Without Conscience*, 203.
24. Hare, 2.
25. Hare, 172.
26. Hare, 196–97.
27. Hare, 202.
28. Hare, 221–22, emphasis added.

Conclusion

1. Valerie Richardson, "Asphyxiation Not the Cause of George Floyd's Death: Autopsy," *Washington Times*, May 29, 2020, https://www.washingtontimes.com/news/2020/may/29/george-floyd-died-police-restraint-combined-health; "Two Autopsies Found George Floyd's Death Was a Homicide," https://www.politifact.com/factchecks/2020/sep/25/blog-posting/two-autopsies-found-george-floyds-death-was-homici/.
2. https://video.foxnews.com/v/6168680803001.
3. Victor Garcia, "Black Lives Matter Leader States If US 'Doesn't Give Us What We Want, Then We Will Burn Down This System,'" *Fox News*, n.d., https://www.foxnews.com/media/black-lives-matter-leader-burn-down-system.
4. Hayek, *Road to Serfdom*, 175, 176.
5. Mill, *On Liberty*, 13ff.
6. Michael Goodwin, "Joe Biden Finally Breaks Silence on Urban

Violence, Too Late: Goodwin," *New York Post,* August 27, 2020, https://nypost.com/2020/08/27/joe-biden-finally-break s-silence-on-urban-violence-too-late-goodwin/.

7. Jordan Greer, "Bucks Players Deliver Statement after Boycotting Game 5 vs. Magic: 'We Are Calling for Justice for Jacob Blake,'" *Sporting News,* August 27, 2020, https://www. sportingnews.com/us/nba/news/bucks-boycott-magic-game- 5-jacob-blake/bqc2c7x6odiu1i3hp2lbzakcr.

8. LeBron James (@KingJames), "And y'all wonder why we say what we say about the Police!!," Twitter post, August 24, 2020, https://twitter.com/KingJames/status/1297979490933645312.

9. Gabrielle Fonrouge, "This Is Why Jacob Blake Had a Warrant out for His Arrest," *New York Post,* August 28, 2020, https:// nypost.com/2020/08/28/this-is-why-jacob-blake-had-a-wa rrant-out-for-his-arrest/.

10. Brie Stimson, "Kenosha Police Union Gives Its Account of Jacob Blake Shooting," *Fox News,* n.d., https://www.foxnews. com/us/kenosha-police-union-gives-its-account-of-jacob-bl ake-shooting.

11. Molly Hensley-Clancy, "Joe Biden Said the Police Officers Who Shot Jacob Blake and Breonna Taylor Should Be Charged," *BuzzFeed News,* September 2, 2020, https://www. buzzfeednews.com/article/mollyhensleyclancy/biden-jaco b-blake-breonna-taylor-police-charged.

12. https://www.secureamericanow.org/cities_defunding_police.

Made in the USA
Coppell, TX
19 July 2021

59168164R00115